Tears, Love

Laughter

Bill and Sil's

Amazing New Zealand Adventure

By

Sylvia Sanderson

Copyright © 2017 Sylvia Sanderson

All rights reserved, including the right to reproduce this book, or portions thereof in any form. No part of this text may be reproduced, transmitted, downloaded, decompiled, reverse engineered, or stored, in any form or introduced into any information storage and retrieval system, in any form or by any means, whether electronic or mechanical without the express written permission of the author.

ISBN: 978-0-244-92638-0

Front cover photograph - copyright Sylvia Sanderson
Design - Astra print of Barrow in Furness

PublishNation
www.publishnation.co.uk

For Teigan, Jaden, Keira, Charlie and Oscar, you have brought light and joy into my life. To those who have loved and supported me, I feel very blessed. Also to those we have loved and lost, but who will never be forgotten. And there's one person I couldn't possible leave out ... my dear friend and partner, Bill.

Acknowledgements

We would like to thank the Francis Camfield Trust, the Pollard and Dickson Trust, the W F Southall Trust, and the Swarthmoor Hall Committee for their support and contributions towards our costs for travelling in the ministry in New Zealand.
Thank you,
—Bill and Sylvia.

A special thanks to family and friends for your support of our amazing New Zealand adventure. And, finally, a big thank you to family, friends, and Quakers in New Zealand. We will always remember your unyielding support, guidance, and friendship.
—Bill and Sylvia.

To adventurers around the world

'Twenty years from now you will be more disappointed by the things you didn't do than the ones you did. So, throw off the bowlines. Sail away from the safe harbor. Catch the trade winds in your souls. Explore. Dream. Discover.'
—Mark Twain.

Table of Contents

i Introduction 1
ii A Brief History of New Zealand 4

Chapter 1: Tears of Farewell and a
Singapore Experience 6

Chapter 2: A Devasted City 15

Chapter 3: Travelling South in Search
Of Penguins 40

Chapter 4: The Sound of the South 50

Chapter 5: Earthquake News 62

Chapter 6: Northwards Bound via
Whale Watching Seas 67

Chapter 7: Sailing to Christmas on the North Island 83

Chapter 8: Summer Gathering in the Chosen Valley 96

Chapter 9: A Journey to Where the Spirits Leap 102

Chapter 10: The Treaty of Waitangi 111

Chapter 11: An Unexpected Journey 122

Chapter 12: Heading to Paradise 128

Chapter 13: Two Cities on the North Island 135

Chapter 14: Steam Valley	141
Chapter 15: The Garden City via Hobbiton	148
Chapter 16: Lake, Thermal Steam, and Raging River	152
Chapter 17: On Course for the Settlement	159
Chapter 18: Sailing South via the Capital City	165
Chapter 19: Mistletoe and Wine	169
Chapter 20: From a Golden Bay to a Frozen Walk	174
Chapter 21: Southern Alps and a Real Scottish Castle	184
Chapter 22: The Church of the Good Shepherd	187
Chapter 23: Christchurch – an Earthquake Experience	190
Chapter 24: Isaac's Last Stand	193
Bill and Sil's 101 Favourite Travel Experiences	200
Bill's Birds (of the Feathered Variety)	203
The Quaker Story	211
Quaker Meeting for Worship	216
Epilogue	217
Bibliography	218

NORTH ISLAND

- Cape Reinga
- Waitangi
- Whangarei
- Tasman Sea
- Pacific Ocean
- Waiheke Island
- Coromandel
- Auckland
- Thames
- Miranda
- Tauranga
- Hamilton
- Rotorua
- New Plymouth
- Taupo
- Whanganui
- Palmerston North
- Wellington
- Picton

SOUTH ISLAND

Tasman Sea

Picton
Wellington
Nelson
Blenheim
Westport
Hanmer Springs
Greymouth
Arthur's Pass
Kaikoura
Pacific Ocean
Christchurch
Fox Glacier
Banks Peninsula
Lake Tekapo
Oamaru
Milford Sound
Dunedin
Te Anau
Invercargill

Introduction

Who would have thought we would be travelling across the two islands of New Zealand in a camper van, and a very small camper van at that? It hadn't even crossed my mind to travel to the other side of the world. I had never even thought about it. Yet here we were, preparing for our departure.

Bill had read the advert for voluntary wardens at the Quaker Centre in Christchurch, New Zealand, and broached the subject with me. It was a definite no from me. Leave my family, my home, my job, and travel to the other side of the world? I couldn't even think about it. Yet it's amazing what a difference a day makes. I had awoken in the night and something was telling me to go for it, now or never … Be adventurous. The following morning, I found myself swayed towards the idea. After all, ignorance is bliss. It's just as well I didn't know what was to happen over the next year or so.

Finally, by August 2010, we had secured the positions of Resident Friends at the Quaker Centre in Christchurch and had set the ball rolling by making plans.

While looking ahead to the following year, and while forming our itinerary, the news came through of a large earthquake in the Christchurch area at a magnitude of 7.1. There was a lot of damage but no loss of life. It was 4 September 2010.

Our hosts in New Zealand contacted us and said everything could go ahead as planned, and were we still willing to travel there in the October of 2011? We didn't flinch. Yes, of course we were, as we were already busy organising our affairs for the journey. In no time at all it was December 2010 and we had applied for visas for a twelve-month stay in New Zealand.

In January 2011, we resigned from our jobs giving three months' notice, as we were to spend the following six months, April to October, visiting family and friends and preparing for our departure. Alas, it wasn't to be so straightforward. The day after we had resigned from our jobs we had word from New Zealand Immigration that our visas had been rejected, on the grounds of lack of support and repatriation, if needed, from our hosts. We were gutted. Our jobs were gone, my house had been sold, and we had thought it was full steam ahead. We notified our hosts and they said not to worry, as they would enquire about the visa situation and see how they could assist us.

Good. We were back on schedule. It was soon February 2011 and we were pushing ahead with our plans. Then we were stopped in our tracks when someone said,

"Have you seen the news?"

On 22 February, 2011, there was another big earthquake in the Christchurch area at a magnitude of 6.3, with more severe damage. And, sadly, much, much worse, this one claimed over 180 lives. We felt numb – inadequate – at so much suffering. We carried on, determined to go to Christchurch. Then the final blow struck, and our plans were in turmoil. We were informed that the cottage we would have lived in was no longer habitable, and the meeting house we were to look after was no longer viable. Our immediate feelings were more of concern for the people in Christchurch: the loss of lives, homes, businesses, and their normal sense of everyday life. Our disappointment was as nothing compared to their situation. We would survive.

We kept in touch with the people of Christchurch Meeting as they looked at other options for us to travel to New Zealand. While pondering over their suggestions we came to the conclusion that we would make the journey, but we would do so under our own steam. So, we put it to our once prospective hosts that we would travel to New Zealand for six months, as no visas would be needed before we left Britain. We would hire or buy a camper van, so as not to be a burden to anyone. We would help, if we could, in Christchurch, whatever that entailed. We would travel the country to other Meetings and to isolated Quakers, which would give us an opportunity to tell the Quaker story, and, of course, take in some of the tourist sights of New Zealand. After all, we were soon to be jobless and homeless.

Time moved on, and by early June 2011 we found ourselves in a now or never situation, but we still felt completely compelled to make the journey. We heard from the New Zealand Quakers, they would be delighted to welcome us and help us where they could.

Then the next shock hit Christchurch. On 13 June, 2011, another earthquake struck the city at a magnitude of 6.3, and even more damage was reported.

Did we still have the initial optimism to make the journey? Christchurch was in tatters. There were aftershocks daily. The people couldn't think straight: they were physically and mentally shattered.

Would we go? Travel into an earthquake zone? We mulled it over for a couple of days, but we really should have talked at length about the situation. Instead, we focused on our plans, especially not to be a burden and to be as self-sufficient as we possibly could. So, with two borrowed rucksacks the journey began, as we busied ourselves readying for our departure in October 2011.

News continued to filter through of more aftershocks, more damage, and more shattered lives.

A Brief History of New Zealand

Aotearoa – The Long White Cloud
The two islands we now know as New Zealand, North Island and South Island, were discovered floating in the Pacific Ocean, covered with deep, dark, dense forests. Their coastal waters were awash with sea lions and seals, and in the deeper waters swam thousands of whales. The islands were isolated but rich, with an abundance of food: a vast, diverse land, with expansive scenery, from snow-topped mountains, glaciers, and geothermal volcanic landscapes, to forests full of wildlife.

In the years around 1200 AD, New Zealand was a land of trees and birds but no people. It was sometime between 1250 AD and 1300 AD that the Polynesians arrived and settled on the islands. These two islands must have been an alluring sight to the Polynesians, who had travelled thousands of kilometres from other tropical places to this fruitful land. They were good sailors, fishermen, and farmers, and had crossed the Pacific Ocean in boats called waka. They brought with them provisions, along with plants and animals, including dogs and rats. The Polynesians realised there was food aplenty on these new islands, as they explored and exploited them ruthlessly. The moa (a native flightless bird) and the seal were an easy kill, so were hunted extensively.

Chiefs were leaders of communities. They had no written language, but communicated with songs, poetry, and drawings, including body markings. They fished and farmed, and burnt the forests to make way for crop growing.

By the sixteenth century both islands had been discovered, and were being used. The Polynesians then began to move further north on the North Island, as the climate was warmer there, and they had a better chance of growing good and plentiful crops. They built towns and villages and pā defences (pā means fortified village), which were usually erected on raised hills or volcanic mounds. The Polynesian settlers were the ancestors of the modern-day Maori, so it must have been quite a shock to these tribes when, later in the seventeenth century, they saw big ships from Europe sailing on what they thought were their waters.

It was in 1642 when Abel Tasman sailed two ships on the seas around the islands, flying the Dutch flag he eventually anchored in Golden Bay. A boat being rowed between the two ships was intercepted and attacked by Maoris, and four sailors were killed. Tasman then moved on.

In 1769, other ships from Britain and France arrived, sailed by James Cook and Jean-François-Marie de Surville. From the 1790s whalers, traders, and missionaries began to arrive and establish settlements. As the British settlers increased, the British government decided to negotiate a formal agreement with the Maori chiefs for New Zealand to become a British colony. A treaty was drawn up in English and translated into Maori. The Treaty of Waitangi was signed on 6 February 1840 at Waitangi in the Bay of Islands. Over the next few months the treaty was taken around the country and signed by some 500 Maori chiefs.

Over the years there has been a lot of controversy over the treaty, thought to be caused mainly by translation problems. Maori believed they had given permission for the British to use the land, but not to take ownership. Disputes over ownership, causing violent conflicts, continued through the nineteenth century. Many of the rights guaranteed to the Maoris in the treaty were ignored.

However, since the 1970s, there has been more respect from successive governments. The Waitangi tribunal was set up in 1975, and some claims brought by Maori tribes were heard. In some cases, compensation was awarded, but disagreements over the terms of the treaty still continue in New Zealand today.

It was in late October 2011 when Bill and Sil took New Zealand by surprise. Arriving with little more than a rucksack each, they were ready to accept the spirit of the Islands, and to hold them and their people with love and compassion. Their upbeat and positive attitude meant they would be a burden to no one, except maybe themselves.

Chapter 1

Tears of Farewell and a Singapore Experience

Our big day had finally arrived, and we were due to leave for New Zealand late in the afternoon. It was also a very emotional day as we prepared to leave family and friends. We were to leave behind the desire to hibernate during the cold winter months of Britain and fly off to New Zealand and into their summer. Leaving my family was very upsetting and I asked them not to come to the train station, as the tears were already flowing. So, late in the afternoon we left for Manchester Airport to stay at the Hilton Hotel overnight, in preparation for our flight to Singapore the next morning.

The Hilton was pleasant and, after a rather expensive although adequate meal, we retired to bed at a reasonable hour in anticipation of our early start. The hotel provided transport to the airport and I had booked this the night before, rather earlier than was really necessary: for 6.45 a.m., to be precise. The next morning, with Bill in tow, muttering and moaning about my obsession for needing to always 'be in good time' (ridiculously early, in fact), we arrived at the check-in desk at the airport, but it was not yet open. There was yet another grumble from Bill as he marched off to find the nearest loo. My 'must get there in good time' attitude would absolutely infuriate him, but at least I could check the passports and tickets one more time before he reappeared. The fact is that Bill is the type who will wander off to the loo as his train is approaching the platform at the train station, but I'm afraid that's just far too much excitement for me.

As we were checking in our luggage it was commented on how light we were travelling for a stay of six months, with just a large rucksack each.

Mmm, I thought. If I'd had my way we'd also have had at least a very large suitcase. Six months living out of a rucksack wasn't sitting too well with me.

After our ever so early check-in I managed to placate Bill with a good full English breakfast, although he wasn't amused when I told him that would probably be the last full English he'd see for the next six months.

"Oh," said Bill indignantly, "so they don't have bacon and eggs in New Zealand ... That's a shame."

"Course they probably do," I retorted, "but we, or should I say I, probably won't feel like cooking the full monty in a camper van."

"I don't want a full monty, just a good breakfast occasionally," Bill replied.

We'll see, I thought, as I realised I was glaring at the people opposite. You see, sometimes this is what I do. Yet I don't realise I'm giving people a sort of haughty look.

At that moment Bill said,

"Why are you giving those people one of your looks?" Little did he know it wasn't really them I could see.

What a wonderful beginning to Bill and Sil's Amazing New Zealand Adventure, although at that stage we hadn't given our journey a name. Oh, what were we doing? Two people who had only lived together over the last few months in a static caravan – and that had been quite challenging – about to spend six months in a camper van ... It was beginning to feel like a recipe for disaster.

We were flying with Singapore Airlines, and our flight was on time. We boarded the aircraft with eager anticipation. After all, this was going to be an experience of a lifetime, wasn't it? We were trying to be very positive, as the intention was to spend quite some time in Christchurch, and we knew that the devastation of the earthquakes was widespread and affecting a lot of lives. So, we carried on, with strength and with determination not to be a burden to these already laden people, and to take as much love and support with us as we possibly could. Then disappointment hit us. We had been looking forward to watching a couple of movies during the long-haul flight to Singapore, but our monitors weren't working, so there was no in-flight entertainment for us.

"Never mind," we said, as we'd taken plenty to read and we could look forward to a couple of drinks and meals. There had been a choice of food on the flight. Bill had booked himself a veggie meal, as he doesn't like eating meat unless it's organic. (I know, I know, what about the big breakfast?) The food arrived, and as Bill was eyeing up my carnivore meal I laughed aloud and said,

"Not a chance," and devoured it with gusto. Lovely.

Singapore

We landed at Singapore Changi airport at 7.15 a.m. There were no problems with passport control or immigration, so we were soon collecting our rucksacks and looking for the desk where our transport had been booked.

Our travel agent had booked us into the five-star Park Inn Clark Quay Hotel for a two-night stopover and we hoped to be able to check into our room as soon as was possible, to enable us to catch up on some rest and sleep. As it happened we had quite a wait at the airport, while a car was organised to take us to the hotel, which was frustrating as we were both becoming slightly tetchy. The airport began to feel cool so we piled on a few extra layers of clothing. As soon as we'd done this our names were called, as our transport had arrived. As we emerged into the street the humidity hit us and we began to strip off those extra layers we'd just put on, much to the amusement of the passers-by. They'd obviously seen it all before.

On our arrival at the hotel we were met at the door by the concierge and the porters. They were very smartly dressed, in white uniforms. We were helped from the car – at least, I was – and then they promptly began to take our rucksacks from the boot. Bill was having none of it. He was quite perturbed, and began this little tussle with one of the porters over his rucksack.

"Thank you, sir," said the porter with a smile on his face, as he pulled at the rucksack that Bill was almost hugging to himself.

"Just let him have your bag, Bill," I said, as I could see that this was about to become a battle of the bags.

"No," retorted Bill. "I can manage."

"Thank you, sir," the porter repeated, and pulled a little harder.

Eventually Bill grimaced and let go.

Oh no, I thought. What's this all about?

After checking in we were told we could have our room straight away ... phew. What a relief, as I was feeling fairly tired. We were then escorted to our room by the lovely young man who had met us outside the hotel, and guess who was carrying all the bags? No, not Bill, much to his disgust.

On the way up I said, rather quietly to Bill,

"Put your hand in your pocket."

"What for?" boomed Bill.

"Shush," I said, pointing to the porter a little way ahead of us. "Money ... him ... you know ... tip." I was hot and tired and becoming quite exasperated. If we couldn't cope with a few bags and go with the flow of the hotel, what use would we be in New Zealand? Bill's face contorted as he put his hand in his pocket and managed to find the smallest coins possible. As the porter held the bedroom door open for us Bill tried to walk in first, but I pushed past him, gave him one of my disdainful looks, and surreptitiously said,

"Skinflint."

We rested for a couple of hours and then freshened up and decided to go and discover Singapore. I didn't really know what to expect. I'd read up a little, but as we weren't going to be in Singapore very long I thought we'd go with the flow, see how we felt. I rather thought of it as a stopover and as resting time. So, wow, what a surprise ... How clean, and tropical, and busy. Apparently, there's very little crime in Singapore, and everyone seemed to have jobs. Chewing gum was totally banned, and throwing litter could attract a fine of around £250. Luckily, we'd been told about the chewing gum ban before we left Britain, so we'd ensured our bags and pockets were totally gum-free.

So, bleary-eyed and with a map in hand, we set off to see as much of this wonderful city as was possible in two days. We took the lift to the ground floor and passed through the reception area, and as we did so the lovely young porter, who had carried our luggage earlier, moved swiftly to the doors and held them open for us.

I walked through and said, "Thank you."

But, much to my consternation and to the amusement of the on looking reception staff and concierge, Bill pointed to the doorway and said, rather too politely,

"No, after you."

Oh, no, I thought, here we go. Game on. I lifted my head high, smiled at the porter, walked back into the lobby, and yanked Bill – ever so gently, of course – by his arm and through the door. Then, to add insult to injury, the porter gave Bill a slight bow. Oh dear. Game definitely on.

We'd had a quick look at the street map in our room and decided that our first ports of call were to be Chinatown and the Buddha Tooth Relic Temple and Museum. The latter was a fascinating building in the architectural style of the Tang dynasty, and it had been built to house the tooth relic of Buddha. The admission was free, and photography was allowed in some areas of the temple. It was glowing red and gold on the inside, with hundreds of Buddhas lining the walls. There was also a very peaceful rooftop garden. It was well worth the visit. As a visitor, you're asked to dress modestly, and to give an offering if you are able to.

We left the temple to stroll around the streets of Chinatown. Brightly lit lanterns adorned the buildings. There was a buzz about the place as people wandered around the stalls that lined the streets, displaying their wares. The wonderful smell of spicy cooking – hot, sweet, and smoky foods – filled the air as we sauntered around. We admired the trinkets, the cheaper goods, and of course the more expensive items. We didn't feel pushed or cajoled into buying anything, like you are in a lot of other tourist areas.

Then the hunger pangs set in as the glorious smells of cooking food pervaded the air. The exotic aromas had certainly worked on our digestive juices. Our travel agent had recommended we eat at a place above the indoor market, which had stalls selling Chinese food.

"Not too sure about that," we had said. But she had reassured us that it was perfectly safe and hygienic.

We found the indoor market and wandered around looking for the food market, which we later discovered was called a hawker centre. Eventually, with a couple of smiles and nods, we were directed to some stairs (we probably looked very much like lost European tourists), and what we found at the top of them was amazing. There, going up and down in straight rows, were over 200 stalls selling different foods. The stallholders cooked in tiny kitchens, and all around were tables and benches and chairs. It was 5.45 p.m., and the place was a hive of activity. The hawker centre was packed with what seemed to be mainly local people – friends and colleagues chatting as they munched their way through their plates of food ... whole families – mums, dads, and children – enjoying a meal together. All we could hear were people chatting in a language we didn't understand, although it did have a loving, friendly feel – just how it should be with family and friends talking about their day over a good meal.

Well, I'll never say no to a Chinese meal, although I won't go as far as hens' claws and that sort of thing. In fact, if you just don't tell me what the contents are, I'm fine. So, with mouths dropped open and probably slightly drooling, we started to wander around the stalls, some selling soups, some selling noodles, rice dishes, and on and on, and some selling things I didn't like the look of ... but we weren't going to mention that, were we?

Our decision was made for us, as we found the only free table and decided to eat from the nearest stall selling rice dishes. We just pointed to some of the pictures of the food and it was no sooner said than done. Just before our meal arrived Bill had espied a beer stall, so with chopsticks in one hand and beer in the other we tucked in to our food and drink. The cost was $4 each (about £2) and the food was by far the best Chinese food I had ever tasted. The stallholders worked in such a small space but were still very friendly and smiley. The stalls and the tiny kitchens appeared to be very clean and apparently were scrupulously inspected for food hygiene, so we enjoyed our food without the worry of a dicky tummy. Fully sated, we made our way outside and back through the busy city. The streets were lit by colourful lanterns, and all sorts of aromas filled our nostrils as we wandered through Chinatown, along the Singapore River, and back to the hotel.

Then the fun began again. I'd forgotten about this and was quite taken aback, as when the porter held the door open for us and walked towards the lift, obviously to retrieve it, guess who wasn't having any of it? Yep, Bill. He charged ahead and, with a big, gleeful smile of glory, pressed the down button on the lift. And so, the game was well into its first half.

The next morning, I knew the game was going to continue, as it became a battle of the doors. We entered the lift to go down to the ground floor, and as we did so Bill obstinately stood right next to the doors to ensure he was the first one out. As soon as the lift stopped, and in the blink of an eye, Bill shot out, straight to the front door, and held it open for me while looking towards the porter with a very cheeky grin. Hang on ... Bill never holds a door open for me.

We decided to take one of the tourist buses around the city, took pot luck, and jumped on to the first one to appear. We arrived at the Botanical Gardens, where we alighted for a quick look around, and intended to jump back on to another tourist bus and carry on sightseeing. However, you just don't take a quick look in the Botanical Gardens of Singapore. There was too much to see, and it was too incredible to miss.

It has been described as 'A Timeless Tropical Eden'. The sixty-three hectares (155.3 acres) are home to a great diversity of tropical plants. We loved the Ginger Garden. We hadn't known that the banana was part of the wider ginger family, albeit a cousin. We were fascinated to be able to walk behind a waterfall and not get wet. We strolled through the rainforest with herbs, ferns, climbers, shrubs, and trees. Oh, and the rainforest was true to its word. We experienced a wonderful tropical storm just after reading the sign saying: *If there's a storm please do not enter this forest*. Great. Too late, as we were right in the middle of it. We ran down the paths like a couple of schoolchildren, giggling all the way, and got absolutely soaked. Apparently, Singapore is one of only two cities with a tropical rainforest within its city limits.

We then moved on to the Evolution Garden, the Eco Garden, the Tropical Orchard Garden, the Poisonous Plant Garden, which you can't actually enter ... Just as well, really, as we wouldn't want Bill getting his hands on anything like that, now, would we? The National Orchid Garden had a collection of more than 1,000 species and 2,000 hybrid orchids. They are beautifully refined flowers, with an air of purity and tranquility.

It had been so easy to lose ourselves in the colourful, thought-provoking, tropical paradise for the day, but then time flew by, and it was soon late afternoon when we realised we needed to catch the first tourist bus that was heading back towards our hotel.

On arriving back to the hotel, I stood back as I remembered that the game was on. I must admit though I was taken by surprise when Bill pushed past me and rushed forward to the door. He didn't even hold it open for me. But then, as he never does, why was I surprised? He then charged in and literally ran to press the lift button, with the porter in close pursuit. Well, I'd never seen anything like it. Guess who was standing on the outside of the hotel looking in through a closed door? Yes, me.

They say, 'Give me the seven-year-old and I'll show you the man'. No. Give me the man and I'll show you the seven-year-old. Sorry, guys.

Evening arrived, and where else would we want to eat but the hawker centre? We strolled through the streets of Chinatown once again, and were still enchanted by the buzz and the oriental smells.

Oh, yes, before we had left the hotel there had been a bit of a tussle at the front door. Bill shot out of the lift and ran to the door, with the porter in hot pursuit. Bill succeeded in reaching the door ahead of the porter. He then turned and, with a gleeful smile, winked at me. Only he was on the outside and I was still on the inside.

I marched through the door, took Bill by the hand and, ever so gently, pulled him back into the hotel as I said, "It would be polite if you held the door open for me." But, to Bill's distress, the porter beat him to it. So, who had the biggest smile then?

We went back to the same stall and managed to find the same seats ... We are creatures of habit, you see. The cook and his wife recognised us from the previous evening. We were probably just about the only Europeans in the place, and they became very interested and wanted to know where were we from and how long we would be staying in Singapore. When we explained as best we could they seemed disappointed that we weren't staying longer. They were obviously very pleased that we enjoyed their food. A wonderful meal yet again ... yum, yum: chopsticks in one hand and beer in the other. It doesn't get much better than that, does it?

We idled our way back to the hotel and enjoyed a glass of wine on the roof terrace next to the pool. It was very relaxing, as we had the whole terrace to ourselves. What a lovely final evening in Singapore.

This was after the cat and mouse show: Bill and the porters yet again. They had certainly fooled Bill this time. When we arrived back at the hotel one of the porters was there at the front door. He held the door open with a big smile and a slight bow. Bill shot through and into the lobby. Oh, calamity. Poor Bill. There, standing by the lift, was another porter with his finger poised over the button. Bill stopped in his tracks and turned back to the door and looked in disbelief. I couldn't stop laughing. Bill's face was a picture. I think we knew who was ahead in the game.

The following day we weren't due to leave the hotel until later in the afternoon and, as our room was available until 2 p.m., we couldn't resist a last leisurely swim and a lounge by the pool in the morning. It was very quiet, and it seemed quite a fitting closure to our short stay at the Park Inn Clark Quay Hotel. We would highly recommend it.

However, it was soon time to leave. There was yet another game with the porter, a tussle with the rucksacks. I don't know what the final score was, but boys will be boys (although I had a sneaking suspicion that they both quite enjoyed the challenge). Then our transport arrived, and we found ourselves being whisked through the streets of Singapore on our way back to Changi Airport and the final leg of our journey to New Zealand.

Chapter 2

A Devastated City

Christchurch
We landed into Christchurch airport at 8.30 a.m. on Saturday, 29 October 2011. How strange it had felt leaving autumn behind and flying into spring. We should have been wrapping up in winter woollies and dragging our extra tog duvets out of storage. Yet, here we were looking forward to another summer. It was a slow process going through immigration and customs, it took about two hours. You're asked not to take any unwrapped food into the country and to make sure your walking boots are clean, but there were some people who obviously didn't take any notice and were being asked to empty their suitcases. We found it unbelievable the items some people were trying to take in. I'll leave that to your imagination! Eventually with our six-months visas stamped into our passports, and with a nervous hesitation, as we really didn't know what to expect, we headed through the airport and on to the arrivals gate, where we were met by a Friend from Christchurch Quaker Meeting.

After some welcome refreshments and a grocery shop stop we headed off to check into our first week's accommodation, Amber Holiday Park, on Bleinheim Road, in the suburb of Riccarton, which was about 4 kilometres from Christchurch city centre. It was early afternoon as we were being driven through the streets of Christchurch, and everything looked pretty normal, business as usual, but then as we surveyed the roads we saw the raised manholes. This was our first experience of earthquake damage, and although it didn't seem too severe this was only the beginning. The manholes in the road had been raised and pushed up, some six to twelve inches, by the pressure of the earthquakes. Most had been leveled off as best possible, but they still caused quite a bump, rather like the sleeping policemen in Britain, the ones on the roads not the ones in uniform.

As we travelled through the streets of Christchurch it became obvious that the earthquakes and aftershocks had left a trail of devastation. When the earthquakes roared through the city some of the streets and roads turned into rollercoasters, or were like waves on the sea, and all anyone could do whilst this was happening was drive up and down with them, or stop, and hope for the best. The pavements and roads had cracked and up came the liquefaction, how terrifying!

(Liquefaction, a process that generates a liquid from a solid. In this case, the soil under the roads had liquefied.)

We didn't experience this, but later people told us how frightening and incredulous it had been. To be driving along a flat even road and then, suddenly, hearing the roaring and rumbling and watch the road as it moved and rolled about.

Sunday morning and we were thankful to have had a very restful night, even though we had discussed the reality of our being in an earthquake zone. We were determined to be positive, and went to the Quaker Meeting for Worship in Christchurch. The meeting was followed by chatting and a lovely bring and share meal. We soon began to feel the tension, as we were told of the devastating damage in the city and outlying areas. Fear in the eyes, bodies held rigid with the stress of everyday living. There wasn't any such thing as normality, this had gone, to be replaced by agonizing thoughts of the next big one!

On the Monday morning, we basked in the spring sunshine as we travelled up to the Banks Peninsula to a Bach (holiday home). There we helped weed the garden. The spring flowers were beautiful, yet we were finding it difficult to get our heads around the fact that it was nearly November. This was good work, as Bill was getting a bit of a gardening fix. He's a keen gardener and outdoor person, so after two days in the city (Singapore), and two days, (well almost with time zones) on an airplane and not forgetting the tension of his game with the porter in the hotel, he was desperately in need of some grounding.

The Banks Peninsula was a stark contrast to the flat plains of Canterbury. Christchurch was supposedly built on swamp land by early settlers. The Peninsula is a rugged, hilly region, with narrow roads along volcanic craters, which were pretty scary to drive along with sheer drops on either side. We had a lovely tour of this peninsula and finished the day with a kumara supper, (fried fish with chips made from sweet potatoes), in the beautiful town of Akoroa.

We were loaned a car for the rest of the week to enable us to travel around the city in search of a campervan, which was to be our home for the next six months. Bill drove, but he hadn't driven an automatic car before so found it quite difficult. We had lots of bumpy stops and starts, until the manager at the camp site where we were staying, told him to sit on his left foot, but thank goodness, he didn't take that advice literally. We visited Christchurch city centre where we began to see some of the devastation the earthquakes had caused. It was quite unbelievable. There had been up to eight thousand aftershocks and tremors to date, and still buildings were falling or being marked as red zone ready for demolition.

We had in such a short space of time been told so much about the devastation of the centre of the beautiful city of Christchurch. Once known as the 'Garden City,' with the River Avon running through the centre and the beautiful Southern Alps in the background. We travelled as far into the city as we could, whilst being safe, to see for ourselves what was affecting these people's lives? We hadn't known what to expect, but from several miles out of the city the impact became visible. The actual centre was cordoned off with high fencing, whilst all the tall buildings were being gently demolished. The debate had begun as to how tall the buildings should be re-built? Some hotel companies were apparently wanting to build fifteen or so storey high hotels, because smaller ones would probably be uneconomical. A re-start programme had already been put into action, which was an innovative and diverse shopping experience. This was bringing people back into the city centre after the closure caused by the earthquakes. Brightly coloured shipping containers had been stacked two high to make temporary shops and cafes. They were very effective. 'Container Mall' proved to be so popular that some wanted to see it continue, even though new permanent developments would appear in the precinct in the future.

It was very clear that there were still hundreds of businesses and homes to be demolished, until the centre would be almost completely flattened.

The cathedral had all but gone. All the brick and stone churches, some with their steeples lying on the pavements, were the first to come down. People had lost their lives, some their businesses, and others their homes. It was very sad to see the devastation, of what had obviously once been, a bustling city.

Despite all of this, there seemed to be a 'calmness' about the place, as people carried on with their day-to-day lives. We spoke to some of the staff in the shipping container shops, and they told us of their yearning for normality, and would we please encourage people back into the city. Yet, they talked of their fears of entering buildings which were two or more storeys high.

We felt moved to acquire a camper van as soon as possible, but the big question was, do we rent or buy? After much debating and gathering of facts and figures, we decided it would be much wiser to rent a van. Buying would have entailed obtaining certificates for self-containment, electric, warranty of fitness, diesel tax etc., and as we were of no fixed abode it would make the paperwork quite complicated. There would also be the pressure of reselling when we were due to leave. So off we set, pen and paper in hand, purse and wallet at the ready.

The first van we saw was lovely, quite big and roomy, but I was very dubious about driving it on some of the narrow roads, as we had agreed to share the driving for the full six months. Also, at $16,000 (about £8,000) it was above our budget, and we wouldn't have been able to keep the same van for the whole term of our stay. We would have had to change the van every couple of weeks or so. Not ideal. Back to our tourist flat and the drawing board. We trawled the Internet until we came across a company called Wendekreisen. Bill e-mailed them and explained what we were looking for, and that it would be preferable to keep the same vehicle for the whole six months, as we planned to travel both the South and North Islands. We received a reply that evening from the Director of the Company. After a couple of phone calls, it was arranged that we would go to their rental site in Christchurch the next morning, to see if they could help us.

The following morning, we met the manager of the Wendekreisen site, which was near Christchurch airport. The MD of the company had already spoken to her, and had asked her if she had any ideas, as most of their vans were already pre-booked. Between them they came up with a plan. For $10,000 (approx. £5,000) they could supply us with a small self-contained van owned by one of their employees in Auckland. The only problem being that it wasn't available for another week, as it would need a 'self-contained' certificate, but in the meantime, they could supply us with another van of similar size.

Self-contained certificate: - A self-contained certificate provides local authorities and communities with a way to recognize that a vehicle poses minimal risk to the environment and public health. This was to enable camper vans and caravans to use reserves and other areas where there are limited facilities. Some of these are Department of Conservation, DoC sites, at a minimal cost of $6 (£3.00) per person but with limited facilities. We had been advised to set up on a holiday park or DoC site, as fines could be very hefty for wild camping in other areas.

So, the deal was done. We would take the temporary van and return it the following week, we would then pick up the van that was to be our home for the next five months and three weeks.

We collected our first van and returned the loaned car back to our friends. I found the camper van very easy to drive and was very pleased we'd chosen a smaller one. Even in the city with all the lumps and bumps and diversions it was quite comfortable. Bill would drive on the way back through the city, and we stopped off for a bit of shopping before heading back to Amber Park. It was raining and we both got very wet diving in and out of the shops. As we drove through the outskirts Bill braked very suddenly, I slid down my seat, feet slamming on the floor of the van. Bill knew of old that I was a very bad passenger, but an excellent back seat driver.

He stopped the van and yelled, "What did you do that for? You didn't have to brake as well, who's driving me or you?"

At which point he got out of the van threw the keys at me and said, "I'm going home."

Oops I thought, I hadn't braked I'd slipped. I got out and said so.

"Oh, Bill come on, get back in the van. I didn't brake I slipped. My shoes are soaking wet. I know we're both a bit tense, and anyway you've a long walk home."

You see, he meant Britain! He really did. Oh dear!

When I turned around to get back into the van I realized we had an audience. They seemed to be enjoying the show, as there, stood on the pavement, was a queue of people waiting at a bus stop. Hands to their mouths obviously trying to stifle their laughter, giggling and smirking. Oh, how embarrassing! What a brilliant start, what good were we going to be to help others?

Bill soon realized he was over reacting and marched back to the passenger seat and said, "You drive."

Oh well, laugh and the world laughs with you. At least that was one day some of the people of this devastated city had something to smile about!

A couple of people from Christchurch Meeting very kindly invited us to their home in New Brighton, a city suburb, for Bonfire Night. There had been a lot of earthquake damage in this area, but the show must go on, and there was to be a firework display on the beach that evening as in previous years.

We said, "Yes, we would love to join them for the evening."

We would park the van on their drive and sleep in it for the first time.

We loaded the van up with all our worldly goods, two rucksacks and some bits and pieces and headed off to New Brighton. We arrived at their house later in the afternoon and could already see some of the damage to the area. They gave us a tour of their home, pointing out all the earthquake damage. Initially, it didn't look extensive, but it was surprising how many hidden cracks and splits had appeared in the walls and ceilings, and most of the doors were askew. This made it nigh on impossible to open some of the windows and doors. They had turned their swimming pool into a garden with pots, and the fish pond into a rockery. There was actually little chance of repair in the near future as they'd been waiting so long for answers from insurers. It was quite depressing for them, and they were really downhearted about it all. However, that morning they had managed to prise the front door open, by chiseling away parts of the frame, and use it for the first time in nine months.

We later had a shared supper and listened to their earthquake stories and the shattering effects on their lives. It was soon time to leave and make our way to the beach to watch the firework display.

On the way some young people, also off to see the fireworks, came running across the road to our male host and said, "Hi Gandalf, look everyone it's Gandalf."

We both looked at him, and found that he did in fact look just like Gandalf, with his hat, long beard and cloak like overcoat. Bill looked on the scene with excitement, but I had to quietly reassure him that it wasn't really 'Gandalf'.

There was a moonlit sky and as we approached the beach we could see silhouettes flickering on the sand and dancing on the water. Then in the distance appeared a throng of people, bobbing along carrying lighted torches and candles, which they held high above their heads. We could hear the sound of chattering and laughter, and the excited voices of children.

It was a lovely mild evening and the fireworks went well. Everyone cheered and clapped, maybe partly from relief that there hadn't been any earthquakes or tremors. It was spectacular, and so well deserved for these people to have some respite and enjoyment. We spent a very comfortable first night in the van and left after breakfast the next morning, with thanks to our hosts.

Bonfire Night or Parihaka Day - New Zealand, 5 November 1881

Te Whiti o Rongomai was a Maori Spiritual Leader and founder of the village of Parihaka.

In 1860 Te Whiti was responsible for saving the lives of the crew and passengers of the ship the Lord Worsely, which was wrecked on the Taranaki Coast, 80 kilometres south of New Plymouth. When Maori threatened the survivors on the beach Te Whiti went to the rescue. He ordered a bullock to be killed and fed the survivors. He later arranged for the survivors to be escorted safely back to New Plymouth.

The legacy by Te Whiti in 1870's

"Though some, in darkness of heart, seeing their land ravished, might wish to take arms and kill the aggressors, I say it must not be. Let not the Pakehas (European settlers) think to succeed by reason of their guns …. I want not war, but they do. The flash of their guns has singed our eyelashes and yet they say they do not want war…. The government comes not hither to reason, but to go out of the way places, they work secretly, but I speak in public so that all may hear".

It has been noted that Mahatma Gandhi referred to the legacy of non-violence taught by Te Whiti.

On the morning of 5 November 1881, some 1600 volunteers and Armed Constabulary troops invaded Parihaka, the largest and most prosperous town in Maori history. More than 2,000 villagers sat quietly by the Marae (meeting house) as a group of children greeted the force led by Government Ministers. The Ministers ordered the arrest of Parihakas leaders, the destruction of the village and the dispersal of most of its inhabitants.

During the illegal arrests and imprisonment, Te Whiti told his people to resist arrest and violence passively saying,

"Go, put your hands to the plough. Look not back. If any come with guns, be not afraid. If they smite you, smite not in return. If they rend you be not discouraged. Another will take up the good work".

At the end of his life Te Whiti stated, "It is not my wish that evil should come to the two races. My wish is for the whole of us to live peaceably and happily on the land"

The community of Parihaka is known around the world as a site of inspiration. There has been a request in recent years, to the New Zealand Parliament, to formally recognize the 5 November each year as Parihaka Day, to commemorate the peaceful resolution of conflict in New Zealand.

We travelled back into the city to attend Meeting for Worship at the Mary Potter Catholic Centre on the outskirts of Christchurch.

The Quaker Meeting House, the Children's room and the Resident Friend's cottage were all, by that time, in the red zone and were due for demolition. Afterwards we chatted with people from the Meeting, but left quite early, as we wanted to visit the Meeting House on Cresswell Avenue, before it was demolished. To see the place where we were to have lived for a year, and to view the enormity of the loss in our fellow worshippers' lives. We had begun to notice that although some buildings looked intact, and not too badly damaged, there was a big problem with liquefaction and the foundations had become unstable.

The soil liquefaction was incredible. This was the cause of most of the building problems in Christchurch, no sewage, no running water, no power etc., but a whole load of mess. As we drove along we noticed a lot of portaloos on the street corners, which were probably being shared by ten to twenty homes. Many places of worship had been severely damaged or demolished, which had a knock-on effect, as this left a shortage of meeting places for voluntary and other community groups.

We decided to leave the city behind for a few days and see how we would survive in our tin tent on wheels. Our intention was never to be a burden. We knew it was important that we stay as safe and as stable as possible. With the force of circumstances all around us, we had become well aware that the occasion may arise when we may have had to make a hasty retreat out of the city. We took this opportunity to familiarize ourselves with campervan living. We would build a routine in the mornings of dumping (grey water and sewage), filling up with water, checking diesel, oil and tyres. We had to be prepared at all times to endeavor not to become a worry to anyone, and be as self-sufficient as we possibly could. This also entailed keeping a good stock of food and supplies. We knew we had to be willing to change our plans if environmental conditions worsened or became intolerable, and for this we had to be well equipped. Every day and every night the threat of even more tremors and earthquakes hung over the city, and the professionals hadn't ruled out the possibility of another 'Big One'!

New Zealanders are very proud of their country and were readily available with advice about some fantastic places for us to visit.

Hanmer Springs had been recommended to us, but of course, as soon as someone mentioned thermal pools we couldn't be held back. We also needed to take some time to catch up on sleep and rest from our journey. Likewise, to digest the tragic events in Christchurch and to come to terms with the fact that, once we were back in the city, there was still a strong possibility of more earthquakes and aftershocks.

Later in the afternoon we headed up State Highway 1 and turned off at Waipara and onto State Highway 7, then a left turn onto a minor road along by the Waiau River and over the Waiau Ferry Bridge. The bridge was extremely narrow with a massive drop on either side. I was driving and I don't like heights so it was eyes closed and hope for the best. No not really. I didn't close my eyes but I rather think Bill did!

We started to see the picturesque scenery of New Zealand. Yet, how could there be such devastation only 140 kilometres away, when in contrast, this was so overwhelmingly beautiful? As we drove towards the Southern Alps we could see the outline of Hanmer Springs all snug and peaceful in the valley. It's a very popular ski resort in the winter months, with lots of holiday chalets, and along with the thermal spas it made for a very good all year-round holiday destination. There was skiing, forest tramps, horse trekking, bungy jumping (not for me or the faint hearted), relaxation in spa pools, and hot water springs. In fact, it had something for everyone.

We booked into the Hanmer Springs Top Ten Holiday Park as we had bought a discount card for these parks, so it seemed a sensible choice.

The next morning, we took our time over breakfast to discuss events so far. We felt it was crucial to be alert without being over tense. Later in the morning we took a walk up Conical Hill, to see and appreciate the natural beauty around us and to live in that moment. It was quite a steep hill with footpaths winding up through the forest and bush, though there were some seats along the way. Bill had already suggested we twitch (bird watch), and was very keen to see as many different birds of New Zealand as was possible, (See Bill's Birds of New Zealand). I love to see birds in their natural habitat, but I really had no inclination to chase them around the forest. Bill's quest began, and there was nothing funnier than watching him dash in and out of the trees on our way up the hill. The culprit was the bellbird. We could hear it, with its melodious bell-like notes, dancing around in the forest from tree to tree and branch to branch. It seemed to be flying around Bill but out of his sight. With his binoculars in hand and stumbling here and there Bill was on a mission. But, by the time we had reached the top of Conical Hill he was becoming quite frustrated and annoyed.

"Where are you? You little beggar," he kept saying over and over.

I carried on sauntering up, admiring the views and the different ferns of the forest. Suddenly, would you believe it, the bellbird appeared behind Bill and was winking at me as if to say,

"Led him a merry dance all the way up. Didn't I?" What a clever little bird.

"Bill look behind you, very slowly," I said.

With his binoculars still glued to his eyes he answered, "Why? I'm busy. I want to catch sight of the bellbird before we go back down." Bill then turned and nearly fell off the rock he was standing on, as he gasped. "Oh, look Sil, quick can you see him?" Ahum!

There was a panoramic viewpoint from the top of Conical Hill with a 360° vista for miles around. There were rolling lush pastures. Pathways lined with yellow flowering broom, which stood out against the dense green of the trees, and the looming mountains in the background.

We had a lovely, much calmer walk back down the hill and admired the broom as we strolled. It certainly was a sight to behold, with its vivid yellow flowers cascading down and around the footpaths. I still found it quite incredible to see the countryside starting to blossom in November. It really was becoming an upside-down world for us.

Later in the afternoon we had a walk around the town to stock up on some fresh foods. Then we went off to the thermal pools, ranging from 29 – 40c in temperature. What bliss!

The thermal resources in this area were discovered in 1859 – but the area was not easily accessible. In the early period, the use of the pools was closely linked to the activities of the Queen Mary Hospital. Recreational bathing, as always, played a large part, but there were other activities such as recuperation of the soldiers returning from the World War I. Relief for arthritic and disabled people also played an important role in its history.

In 1897, the government built an accommodation house described as a sanatorium, and a hotel called The Lodge also opened close to the springs.

1911 – The sanatorium grew to accommodate 18 patients, but was later destroyed by fire on the day that World War I broke out.

1916 – The first block of the Queen Mary Hospital was built near to the pools – this was after Hanmer Springs became the site for the South Island military hospital, and was later to become the rehabilitation centre for sufferers of alcohol, and drug abuse on the South Island.

2003 - The centre was closed.

2008 - The New Zealand Department of Conservation bought the premises.

www.hamnersprings.co.nz

It has since been transformed into leisure pools and a spa. You could sit and relax, and gaze at the redwood trees and mountains towering above, while the natural thermal water eased and soothed any aches and pains.

On Tuesday, 8 November, we drove down State Highway 7 heading back to Christchurch. We were to call in to have supper with two Quaker Friends, who lived in Kaiapoi, some 17 kilometres north of Christchurch. As we had the day to travel, we looked for any interesting places around the area. I really don't know how we fell upon Flaxmere Gardens as it was a short detour from Hanmer Springs off State Highway 7, and about 10 kilometres from Harwarden on Westenras Road. Upon arriving there we were told that the gardens were closed but that they were very happy for us to have a little look around, which ultimately became one of the longest 'little look arounds' we'd ever done.

The website begins with: -

"Relax and be inspired by wonderful vistas that connect you with nature and the rhythm of life, in a garden for all seasons."

It was a private garden and the creation of Penny Zino. A country garden that was formal, informal, woodland, with roses,

rhododendrons, and an immense use of water which created five ponds. There was a large selection of native plants indigenous to the area, a wonderfully peaceful place, idyllic for birds and wildlife. It was a truly interesting and beautifully cared for garden. The weather wasn't great as there were several rain showers, but it didn't spoil the beauty of Flaxmere. Booking apparently is essential and there is also a cottage for rental as well as a facility for weddings.
www.flaxmeregarden.co.nz

We returned to State Highway 7 and as it was nearly lunchtime we wanted to find a beach to park up and raid our little fridge, oh and of course, not to forget that Bill would want mug after mug of tea as one is never enough. We travelled as far down as our destination for the night, Kaiapoi, and found Pines Beach, where we had lunch and a good walk.

We travelled back to Kaiapoi, which takes its name from the Maori pa (meaning fortified village). It was a lovely place with the river Waimakariri flowing through the centre of the town. We later had an interesting evening talking to our hosts about the earthquake news of Christchurch. She worked in the city centre. Her company had had the trauma of moving further out of the city as their building was no longer safe to work in, if at all still there. We had a lovely meal and a glass of wine, which we much appreciated. We later hooked the camper van up on their drive for the night. They had an electric hook up in their garage for their own caravan, so it was ideal. The next morning, we said our goodbyes with a big thank you for their hospitality, and hoped to see them at the Christchurch Meeting later in the month.

We drove back to Christchurch and checked into Amber Park as we were due to swap the vans over later in the day. At last, by mid-afternoon, we had our new van, which we were to call home for just over the following five months. It had been brought all the way down from Auckland for us, and had achieved its self-contained certificate, hooray! This didn't mean we could camp just anywhere. We still had to stick to authorized Campsites and DoC sites and not go wild camping.

On the Thursday, there was a big agricultural show in Christchurch which Bill was keen to attend. I dropped him off there for the day, and set off back to the site to work out what I thought we may need for the van. Small things like a cheese grater, colander, a piece of rug for the floor, as we'd discovered with our first van, if we had wet feet the space became a wash with water and very slippery. Soon, I was having a field day in a massive second hand warehouse, just down the road from the caravan site. There wasn't that much room for more "stuff" (as Bill would say) so I had to reckon carefully how we could reorganize the van. Oh yes, we needed proper mugs for tea, and beer and wine glasses.

I'd just got sorted when Bill arrived back from his day at the agricultural show. Delighted with our now better-equipped "Wendy house" - girls have toys as well as boys - I began to show Bill my finds. Not being a very domesticated person he was none too happy, I can't say what he said but the words, show van, and pointless come to mind. Ah yes, but just wait until he wanted a beer, as he didn't like drinking out of bottles! I may just have found him a glass! Mmm! Then, I waited and watched as Bill started to produce his finds, a cheese bag. A what? I rest my very practical case!

Having managed the first van very well, we would test our survival skills once again in the new van somewhere close to Christchurch, I nearly said home, as this was how it was beginning to feel, bumps and quakes and all. They do say it's the people that make the place, oh how true that was becoming.

We travelled to Spencerville on the Friday, a small semi-rural town on the east coast, north of Christchurch, to see how our newly contained wee home, our tin tent on wheels, would stand the weekend. We named the van Isaac, as we believed it belonged to someone called Isaac in Auckland. We stayed at the Spencerville Beach Holiday Park, a very large site, which we had expected to be very busy being the weekend, but it was relatively quiet. On the Saturday, we walked north along the coastal path from Spencerville to Brooklands. It rained all day. No, it poured all day, and we got soaked. Wet feet and soggy sandwiches on the beach, tremendous fun! We were amazed to see earthquake damage all the way up the coast to Brooklands. They appeared to have taken a real battering. Wet feet and soggy sandwiches didn't seem too bad after all.

I think it may have been the first time I'd seen black swans as I couldn't recollect seeing any before, but they seemed to be an abundance of them and not a white swan in sight, or maybe we just didn't come across any.

Isaac was great. We were both delighted with his performance, and found it was very comfortable even in such a small space. Though after all, he had been so well kitted out and organized, hadn't he?

Earthquake News

On Sunday, 13 November we travelled back to Christchurch and attended Meeting for Worship. After the meeting we shared tea, coffee and biscuits and talked to people about their earthquake problems. It was the same for most, buildings in the red zone, or due for inspection. Some homes had been repaired, and then after the next earthquake they were told that their newly repaired homes were in the red zone, and due for demolition. The problems went on and on and the tensions rose. Every bump or loud noise was taken very seriously, as it could be the next big earthquake. They talked to us about no longer being able to make decisions. Confusion at the thought of their future, and the ever-changing plans by the Government and the Insurance Companies. The sort of pressure that couldn't be imagined, unless you were in their situation, as it was just so immense.

The devastation of the earthquakes and after-shocks was incredible. Most of the city centre was being demolished. The tramlines disappeared through tall fences and into the red zone. The loss of people, buildings, stability, the known, and their dreams, had all been destroyed. Someone had to wait for weeks to identify his wife's body. She was killed in the CTV building. The centre of Christchurch was so badly damaged, that many landmarks/buildings were due to be pulled down. Grief lay just below the surface. Sleep was difficult, so these people were weary, less patient, more easily frustrated, and concentration was poor.

As we spoke to different people it was the same over and over.

"This is trauma – a huge emotional shock – it is eating into our lives – it hurts and plays with our very being. We need tenderness and kindness, a listening ear, but not to comment or judge. We are depleted of all our energies and just when we think it can't get any worse the rumbling starts once again. Is this the next big one?

We don't have any reserves left. We are living and working one day at a time. The simplest daily tasks have become difficult and arduous. We are in a terrifying, un-safe and trembling place.

Please hear our voices. Please hold us in your prayers. Please have hope for us that we may one day live normal lives again."

The stories continued. We did our best to listen and have compassion, but how can you relive someone else's experience in this climate of fear and stress.

We were due to present our first session of the Quaker Testimonies in the evening, but had become quite nervous. Who were we to talk to people about Testimonies when their lives had been turned upside down? So, when we arrived at the venue we were very surprised to see so many attend, twenty-three in all, which considering the circumstances we thought was pretty good. We had a lovely shared meal to begin with, and enjoyed meeting yet more people. We started with a discussion about each testimony, and felt there was a hint of defensiveness in the room. We were very wary, as we had been told 'not to tell Kiwis how to run their lives or their country.' I suppose this initial atmosphere was to be expected, and we would probably have hit the same situation at home in Britain. I explained it wasn't about telling anyone how to run or not run their lives, but to remind us all of our Testimonies, and that we can only do the best we can with the tools we have. It soon livened up and became a wonderful evening of learning from each other. Bill asked those who would wish to, to put under each Testimony a post-it note explaining how they had practiced each Testimony of late. It could be something so small or simple. (You know what they say, if you think small doesn't make a difference, then spend a night under a net with a mosquito. Ouch!) No names, just words, and then we all read them. It was amazing when they grasped the fact that they were actually working very hard to fulfill the Testimonies. Under such difficult circumstances, they hadn't realized their lives were continuing as normally as was possible.

Testimonies: -   S. T. E. P.

Simplicity: Try to live simply. A simple lifestyle freely chosen is a source of strength. Do not be persuaded into buying what you do not need or cannot afford. Keep yourself informed about the effects your style of living is having on the global economy and environment. Simplicity towards inner peace. Live simply so that others may simply live.

Truth: Speak truth to all including those in positions of power. Be truthful in all aspects of your life. Let your yes be yes and your no be no. The truthfulness of the spirt is unending and unchanging.

Equality: Social and Spiritual Equality. Hold no prejudice towards anyone of any race, creed, status or gender. Ensure all groups and individuals are treat with the same respect as one and another. Practice honesty and fairness in all dealings in your daily lives.

Peace: War is not acceptable. Before all wars find a peaceful non-violent resolution. Be at peace with yourself and the world, and those around you will also find peace.

We all could do with watching our STEP.

Bills final note of the evening,

"Now look around at each Testimonies poster. As you read the notes remember that what you see there is the collective activity of the meeting, which will have greater effect on society than each of us as individuals. Rejoice in the strength of the meeting, and then think of others, in New Zealand, working in this way and the impact you have on your nation."

We spent the night at Amber Park and then travelled over to a Friend's house some kilometers out of the city, where we were to stay in their 'sleep out' which had a hot tub in the barn right next to it. We chatted about the effects of the earthquakes. It was momentous for everyone. We just listened and felt pretty helpless. We were soon to realize that listening, and hearing people unburden their stories of trauma and fear, was help in itself.

We bathed in the hot tub the next morning, how lovely. Later in the day we went off to help harvest some asparagus, which were growing in two paddocks just along the road from the house. After all, we were there to help in any way we could. We spent two days harvesting the asparagus, some of which was sold, and any that was left went to the City Mission or the Salvation Army to help feed those in need.

The following day we met four members of Christchurch Meeting to discuss our co-clerking (Co-Chairing), of a Quaker Threshing Meeting. This was to help the Meeting discern which way they were going with the decision for a new place of worship. Buy/build - co-share with another church group or continue to rent? There had been so many earthquakes and after-shocks that people were finding it difficult to think straight and make decisions. We all envisaged a controversial and quite hard to clerk meeting, so we were briefed. We then felt it was time to rest elsewhere for a few days, to clear our thoughts, so as not to have any opinions or discolored vision.

We ventured off to Akaroa on the Banks Peninsula, to stay over this time and see the charms of a sea flooded, huge, old volcanic crater. We spent two days at the Top 10 Holiday Park, which was set on top of a gently terraced hillside, with stunning views across the harbour, overlooking the French themed settlement of Akaroa. It was an excellent site with only a short walk down the hillside to the town.

We avoided talking about the Threshing Meeting, as we needed to keep our heads clear, to help us to discern the situation. We would discuss how we were to clerk the meeting on our return to Christchurch, and only on the day of the actual meeting.

The next day we booked a sea cruise. Off we set, with sunglasses on, and binoculars in hand, we hoped to catch sight of some of New Zealand's sea life. Whilst waiting for the trip there was an earth tremor. I had thought it had just been a wobbly seat in the loo. You know, the type that makes you feel as though you're going to end up on the floor! When I caught up with Bill, he had been sat by the harbour reading.

"That was an awful wobbly loo seat in there. I was rocking and rolling all over the place." As I put the motion into action.

Bill gave me a perplexed look, "Sylvia please don't exaggerate." He seemed to be oblivious to everything going on around him!

Maybe travelling around in our little van, and my excellent driving had made him less aware of any shakes or wobbles. When we joined the queue for the boat trip, the staff were asking if everyone was ok, and did we feel the last tremor. Bill hadn't felt a thing, and I honestly thought it was the loo seat that had been wobbly. The locals were permanently on red alert, feeling every bump and shake however small, all the time waiting for the next big one. The tremors had become part of their daily lives, but that's not to say they were getting used to them. In fact, people in the whole area, and for miles around, were so tense and afraid of what may happen next, that they would jump at the slightest of movements.

The sea cruise was quite uneventful, so it needed to be, as there was enough happening on land. However, the scenery was beautiful and we did manage to see one hector dolphin, which is only about a metre long, lots of seals and several blue penguins. Bill was happy to log his sea life.

After the boat trip, we walked around the quaint, French themed town of Akaroa and wished we could stay longer, to explore some of the gardens and galleries. The French influence was reflected by some of the names, Rue Lavard, Rue Jolie, L'Aube Hill Res; as well as the usual well used English names of Beach Road, Church Street and William Street. Now where did that one come from?

For our last evening in Akaroa we just couldn't resist another kumara fish and chip supper, on the harbour front, absolutely delicious. Little did we know we'd be back!

Akaroa was originally the domain of a Maori chief, but in 1838 the French arrived and thought it was an ideal place to settle and traded goods with the Chief, for what they thought was gaining the whole Peninsula. They later sailed back to France to collect more people and provisions, but when they returned the English flag was flying and it had already been colonized. William Hobson had been sent in the role of Lieutenant Governor over all the land that could be purchased and just six days later the French had arrived back. The French decided to stay and make it as much theirs as possible. Some of the French architecture survived and today some of the streets, restaurants and boutiques have French names.

Sadness in Sumner

It was Sunday, 20 November and we were back in Christchurch staying at a site in the quiet suburb of Bromley. The camp site was quite nice, but had quite a few semi-permanent/permanent campers, so a little bit noisier than the usual and somewhat parochial. Friends of Christchurch Meeting were going to worship outside the old Meeting House in Cresswell Avenue, as a final farewell before the site was to be demolished. It was very upsetting for them, and we didn't feel we could intrude upon this part of their spiritual journey, so we'd decided to go to a small house group Meeting in Sumner. We knew Sumner had been severely affected by the earthquakes and tremors, and wanted to offer our support to this small group.

Sumner is a coastal seaside suburb of Christchurch, it's the first bay on the northern side of the Banks Peninsula, facing Pegasus Bay and the Pacific Ocean. Sumner was badly damaged in the 6.3 magnitude earthquake in February 2011, and what we saw on our drive into Sumner confirmed this damage. It was quite unbelievable. As we drove along the bay, where the blue waters shimmered and glistened in the sunlight, we could see the damage. The roads had makeshift repairs. The rock cliff had collapsed and it was obvious that many homes had been evacuated. Shipping containers had been stacked to make a double wall along the roadside, to stop any more rock fall doing damage. Houses along the way had been abandoned, giving the place a feel of the 'Marie Celeste'. Some houses were literally hanging over cliff edges. There were holes in the road, and places coned off which looked ok, but were obviously very dangerous.

We eventually found the home of the house group and arrived feeling rather sombre and humbled. We joined the Meeting of six elderly Quakers. It was a very silent meeting. No ministry, for which they later thanked us, as they needed some quiet time amid all the anxiety and noise. Whilst we shared tea, cake and biscuits I asked them of their experiences of the earthquakes, and how their lives had changed. I don't think we were prepared to hear what they had to say. Would anyone be, at any time? They were all obviously devastated, as none of them were likely to see their houses repaired and back to normal in their lifetime. This was so sad. I can't describe how I felt for these brave people. They were realists and knew what was ahead of them. I was choked. Yet we continued with the conversation, and they seemed glad to be able to open up and talk to us. We were seeing the same everywhere we went in the Canterbury area. Most wanted to talk and tell us their story.

This group of people in Sumner had been digging holes in their gardens to use as toilets in the night, as the portaloos were down the street. They hadn't wanted to leave their homes and go out into the dark. They felt safer in their own homes, and felt blessed and grateful that they were able to move back in so soon after the earthquakes, even though some of their homes were still very badly damaged. They told us of the mess after a big earthquake, when everything from the cupboards, drawers etc., was strewn all over the floor, all broken and smashed up. Books, TVs, tables, and chairs had been thrown across the room. The frustration of not being able to clean up afterwards, as there were no utilities. Having to find somewhere else to sleep. How it was absolutely terrifying been woken at 4.30 in the morning with the most horrific rumbling noise of the earthquake. The piercing sound of car and house alarms, and the whole house shaking, rocking and rolling.

"What did you do?" I asked.

"I crept about in the darkness to find the nearest doorway and crouched underneath hanging on to the frame, and prayed, and hoped it would soon stop. (Apparently, a doorway is one of the safest places.) It was pitch black and all I could hear was the continuing rumbling, and roaring, and the noise of the alarms and sirens all around me. I was petrified."

We were told of a nursing home where the patients had held hands with the staff, being perfectly calm, they had managed to placate the staff. It seemed they had nothing to lose, and were more concerned for their carers than themselves. Most of the patients died soon after being rehabilitated into their new care homes. They were very brave.

We sat in silence, as they re-counted how they felt and of their fears for the future. As I looked around the room, I saw modest, but strong people, with a resilience that helped them to carry on. We said our goodbyes and wished everyone well. They said they were so pleased we had spent the morning with them, and thanked us for listening so unobtrusively.

We drove back to Christchurch in disbelief and silence. With tears in our eyes, we both counted our blessings, and hoped and prayed for some relief for those involved in disasters around the world.

Supporting Container Mall

We were back in Christchurch and Bill was becoming frustrated because he couldn't get on line. As I always seemed to be busy on the laptop writing our blog, "Bill and Sil's amazing New Zealand Adventure" or downloading photographs.

The next day into Christchurch we would go, to give some financial support to this devastated city with some retail therapy. Our main aim and purpose was to stay positive and bright. On the face of it, it was difficult, so we worked hard to keep our spirits intact. We would laugh at the most ridiculous moments, usually at ourselves. Along with holding everyone in our spiritual light, we soon realised that in the very early days of our journey, this had become our coping mechanism. The last thing the people of Christchurch needed was any negativity.

Were we afraid there might be another big one whilst we were in Christchurch? No! We had nothing to fear but fear itself. We hadn't been involved in any of the big earthquakes, so we had no experience of the fear others held. I don't know how, but we didn't think of the risk we were taking, our spirits just seemed to lead us on.

As it turned out our retail therapy became a very expensive jaunt. Bill bought an iPad and I saw a much better camera than the one I already had, as I had decided that the sights in this wonderful country, deserved to be shot with a good piece of equipment.

And so, the iPad saga began. The sales assistant in the shop said to Bill, "Just switch it on and it's all there." But it wasn't long before Bill and the iPad had fallen out, big time, as it wasn't all there!

Christchurch Quaker Threshing Meeting

Tuesday, 22 November and Christchurch Friends were holding a Threshing Meeting to discern the way forward for the Quaker Meeting. We had been asked to facilitate and clerk this Meeting to enable the Clerks of the Meeting to take an active part.

We needed some space and peace earlier in the day and found a lovely secluded beach near New Brighton, where we could work and find some appropriate words for the Meeting later that evening.

The Meeting

The agenda for the meeting:
- A shared silence with a reading.
- A first threshing session
- A break for tea
- A second session to pull our discernment together in a written minute, which would be forwarded to the Monthly Meeting.

We wrote these notes and were determined to help by clerking the meeting with simplicity, truth, equality and peace, and so this is what Bill read at the beginning of the meeting.

"We are, even as a Threshing Meeting, conducting ourselves as a spiritual, loving, worshipping group.

If you would like to speak –
- Please stand and wait to be called by the clerks before speaking.
- Please leave a short silence between contributions.
- Please speak only once until others, who wish to speak, have done so.
- Please listen deeply and lovingly to each other, and be guided by the light within when you speak and as you listen.

Thank you, Friends."

"We are here this evening to seek to work together through the leadings of the Spirit. To balance the need to move ahead in a timely fashion and for everyone to be included in the process. To search for a way to put your goals, and visions, for a spiritual home into practice.

Your present state is that you had agreed a clear vision at Cresswell Avenue, (the site of the old meeting house), but the earthquakes have prevented you from implementing this. We now need to find a spiritual way forward for your vision.

For this we need to consider do you buy/build, co-own/share, or rent?

Which option will allow you to serve your vision;

To provide for: -
- Your children
- Young Friends
- Yourselves as a worshipping community
- And your wish to engage with and reach out to the local community

Our goal this evening is for us to agree a minute on the way forward. You have all been through a lot. This will influence you, but let it not govern or preclude you from acting as a Meeting. Your personal stories and needs are important, but this is not the forum for sharing them. We are here this evening for the meeting as a whole.

Let us look for the spirit to guide us in an open, loving and sharing way for the Meeting. At the end of this evening we will draw up a minute, which will be agreed and forwarded to Monthly Meeting in December."

We felt the Threshing Meeting went very well. Bill and I shared the clerking in a fairly strict 'right ordering' fashion, which enabled Friends to discern and come to a decision they would all be happy with. It had been so hard for them, as they all had their stories of the earthquakes and that of families and friends. We finally arrived at a minute to which everyone was accepting. There was then a big sigh of relief, and everyone lovingly clasped each other.

Later in the evening Bill met a man from South Africa, and discussed the problems he was having with the iPad. Being an IT man he said he could possibly help. So, there we were, after the meeting, three of us squashed on the front seat of the campervan at 10 o'clock at night, outside the BT shop in the middle of Christchurch trying to get a signal on the iPad. We received odd looks from passers-by, maybe they thought we were about to make a heist! With not much joy and a promise to meet at his house the next morning, we went off to stay in a friends' sleep out for the night.

We were quite exhausted, but exhilarated that the meeting had gone so well. The tension had been immense, and we knew we had to be so careful with our emotions.

The following morning, we were made to feel very welcome at Bill's new found friends home and he soon sorted Bill and the iPad. Thank goodness! Maybe there'll be no more tantrums now, and iPad and Bill can stay happily together. He told us that he was a Hindu, who had been attending the Quaker Meetings as he was enjoying the silence. He was from South Africa and Kenya, but was at that time settled in New Zealand and loving it along with his wife and teenage children. They had arrived just before the first earthquake, so it had all been quite an awakening experience for them.

Chapter 3

Travelling South in Search of Penguins

Oamaru

We were leaving Christchurch for a while to visit other Quakers and places on the South Island. We were very relieved that our time in Christchurch had been so well received, after all we had said we wouldn't be a burden as they had enough to contend with, to say the least. But alas, Isaac had developed a drip, he was beginning to dribble grey water as we drove through the outskirts of Christchurch. Oh dear, weeing in the street is not permitted, so we booked him into Wendekreisen, where they lovingly checked his plumbing.

We hadn't even left Christchurch and Bill started to sing,

"♫Back on the road again, da do do da da♫". (Canned Heat, 1967).

He was quite out of tune, but it was just about bearable, although I hoped it wouldn't continue for too long!

We were heading south on State Highway 1 to Oamaru and the penguin colonies. We were amazed on the way down, how some roadside cafes offered free cups of tea or coffee, there were big signs encouraging you to stop and enjoy their free refreshments. Now, we wondered, was this a ploy to get you through the door and once in there be tempted to buy food? Or, were they genuinely looking after motorists, in case of tiredness, and to help prevent accidents. I think possibly the latter. What a bummer as we never felt we had the time to find out, or maybe that was because I was driving, and I did find it awfully hard to stop once on the road.

Bill went into raptures of delight as we drove over the Rakaia River Bridge, New Zealand's longest bridge with a length of 1.75

kilometres. He made such a racket that I nearly crashed the van, but at least it stopped him singing!

We arrived at the Oamaru Top 10 Holiday Park later that afternoon, and as it was raining quite heavily we decided to do a bit of shopping, bed down for the night and visit the penguin colonies the next day. We awoke the next morning to a lovely spring day. We could hear birds singing and so continued our weekly, name that bird, whilst we tried to identify the birds that were singing or tweeting. After a quick breakfast and a while planning our day, we walked into the town of Oamaru, famous for its Victorian boomtown buildings (now part of the city's heritage), and its penguin colonies. On the way, we strolled through a park which was adjacent to the campsite. It was a lovely walk. The spring flowers were in full bloom and the wispy gentle spring breeze was making the trees and bushes lean and sway. Meandering down one of the footpaths we came across an aviary, which housed some parakeets, or some such parrots. As I was feeling refreshed and quite energetic, I told Bill I could probably get the birds to dance, and copy my movements.

"Don't be silly," he scoffed, "no you can't."

When will he learn that sometimes you just don't challenge a woman....? Oh, but yes, I did. As I moved my head from side to side and hummed a tune one of the birds began to copy me, and as I moved along the front of the cage and bounced my head it followed, imitating my movements.

Bill stood with his mouth dropped open.

"Blimey," he said, "how did you know it would do that?"

To which I replied rather cockily, "It's easy watch," and I carried on performing whilst the bird copied my movements.

Then I heard the laughter, and when I turned around there were quite a few young people watching my performance, they were very amused. Oops! Caught out, very embarrassed. I then tried to explain that I didn't always dance and sing to birds.

They laughed. "Yea, right!"

We beat a hasty retreat from the park and headed for the town centre.

We sauntered around the lovely town of Oamaru, looking at the white stone buildings, which are reportedly some of the best-preserved heritage in New Zealand. In the late 19th century it had been a boomtown with gold mining, quarrying and timber milling. We admired the elegant stone buildings, made from local limestone, as we wound our way along the streets to the waterfront. We stopped to have a cup of tea and a bite to eat in one of the quaint little tea rooms. It was all very easily paced and relaxing, a friendly feel to this area, although New Zealanders are friendly full stop!

In the afternoon, we visited the blue penguin colony, where we peered through the holes into their nests, and saw the chicks waiting for their parents to return and the food they would have with them. It was a purpose built 'natural habitat' and was used as a place of safety for breeding, although the adults still went out to sea every day. We met a very pleasant and informative guide, who told us of a colony of yellow eyed penguins on Bushy Beach. She advised us to go up after 4 p.m. and watch for the penguins walk up the beach from a special viewpoint.

We booked tickets for that evening, to see the blue penguins arrive back to their colony. We then made a hasty retreat, it was just after 3.30 p.m. and we needed to go to Bushy Beach viewpoint in the van, as it was a little too far to walk to get there in time. We eventually reached the viewpoint, (via Bushy Beach Road) although we did get just a tad lost, due to my atrocious navigational skills, but more of that later. As we wandered along the viewpoint people were starting to gather, with the same intention as ourselves, to see the yellow eyed penguin walk out of the sea. Wow! Would it be possible? There was certainly an air of expectation all around, as we all craned our necks over the fence and scoured the beach. Oh and of course, we all kept others right, as even though there was a specific sign stating, *please do not go onto the beach after 4p.m.*, there were those who seemed intent to do so. Not with this crowd around they weren't though!

Bill was rushing along with binoculars to his eyes, tripping over this and that stone or cobble, occasionally bumping into people in his desperation to see a penguin. Thank goodness for my new camera with its zoom lens. Jackpot, there was one waddling out of the sea and along the beach looking weary and tired. I got a shot and couldn't believe it. In my excitement, I went running off to find Bill.

I just didn't want him to miss this awesome sight. A yellow eyed penguin, yea, ok we've all seen them in the water parks and on television, but this was in its own habitat, waddling up the beach Charlie Chaplin style, incredible.

Bill really didn't think I would see one before he did, because I just had a camera, but he had binoculars. When he saw the photograph, he chased after me to where I'd been standing.

I felt like a celebrity as people were asking me, "Did you get a shot? Really! Wow!"

The next moment is one I will never forget. A lone penguin came out of the sea and stood there spreading its wings out in the early evening sunshine. Apparently, they do this to allow the sun to dry them off. Then it began to look agitated and wandered back down to the sea. There it was, stood alone, gazing out to the horizon. It turned and started to waddle back up the beach again. Then it must have changed its mind, as it stopped, looked around and heavily trundled back to the edge of the tide. Out of the sea came another penguin, it waddled up to the first one, they just stood there looking at each other and then there was some sort of an exchange. Wings were flapping, and then suddenly the first whacked the other one across the face. They looked like they were having a right old barney.

"Where've you been? I've been back ages."

"Oh! Keep your wings together I'm back now, what's all the fuss about?"

"Yes, you just take your time, the kids are starving and you're playing around out there."

There they were like two little people, husband and wife, coming home after a hard day's work at sea and exhausted. These wonderful flightless birds, with their distinctive tuxedo-like appearance waddled up the beach together, they would have been at sea all day trying to catch enough fish for themselves and their young, so I guess these two were a pair. I shot some great pictures here, it was just unbelievable, kind of surreal.

After all the excitement, we headed off back to the blue penguin colony, where we took our seats in the grandstand. The blue penguin is the smallest of their kind, they grow to an average of between 13 and 17 inches and have slate blue plumage.

The guides were very strict and asked everyone to be as quiet as possible, because if the blue penguins are disturbed they may go back off to sea and not feed their young. It was definitely no photographs, as the flash can blind the penguins for several minutes and may cause them to have an accident. As always, someone had to be the loudest, and of course someone else had to sneak around trying to take photographs. They were told and even instructed that they would be asked to leave, but to some nothing mattered but that shot.

They began to come ashore in "rafts". It was amazing to see over 150 of these little guys clambering over the rocks to get back into the colony to feed their young. What the penguins didn't know, but we did, was that there had been a very large seal lying at the top of the rocks all afternoon, and he was still there in the evening. We had enquired with the guide about it and she said it could just be resting or it could be ill, it would be left, as they didn't interfere with nature. I felt quite sad about this and wanted to fix him, but knew it would be impossible. The penguins began to clamber over the rocks, but then they took fright as the seal lifted his head and gave a big sigh... Oh dear, this caused them to scamper back onto the rocks, falling over each other, off back down, sideways and every which way, and some just rolled head over heels. A minute or two later they started to venture back up the rocks, ever so quietly this time, putting their heads down as they tried to sneak past the seal. Once past they ran like the clappers, little legs waddling as fast as they could, pushing and shoving each other to get through the specially adapted holes in the fence, and into the colony.

Then the next raft of blue penguins emerged from the sea, sorted themselves out, and made their advance towards the colony and here we go again. Mr. Seal would raise his head, give out a big sigh and a puff, and the penguins retreated, falling over each other and clambering back down the rocks. If this had been an animated movie it would have been quite funny. But, this was the real world, and if they didn't get into the colony they would go back to sea and their young would be left unfed.

Earlier in the afternoon as we had approached the Penguin Visitor Centre we noticed a sign on the road, *Penguins Crossing. Slow.*
We thought it was quite funny, penguins crossing, I don't think so, maybe it was some sort of gimmicky marketing. How wrong we were. Later that evening, as we left the centre, we were asked to be very careful and to look under the parked cars and vans just in case there were any blue penguins wandering around. Lo and behold, as we approached the car park there were little blue penguins scampering around under cars, on the pavements, trying to cross the road, and of course there were some people who just had to take photographs. It was so annoying, shame on them. The sign was genuine after all and penguins were crossing. We checked under our van and had to be patient whilst two penguins waddled out. They were so cute; I could have put them in my pocket. It had been a truly amazing and unforgettable afternoon and evening. What a fantastic experience, it was then we knew we had so aptly named the blog, 'Bill and Sil's Amazing New Zealand Adventure.'
www.penguins.co.nz

We left the camp site the next morning, check out time at most sites was 10 a.m., so it was up, breakfast, shower, fill with water, dump waste water and sewage, and do the usual checks before leaving. We were to call back into Oamaru as Bill wanted to visit the Steam Punk Exhibition. This was a mixture of contraptions and bizarre machinery, using copper, gears, pipes, gas cylinders. It was arranged by a group of creative artists, who collaborated in using Victorian mechanical ideas, scrap and their sci-fi imaginations. It set out to portray an industrial version of steampunk, with a giant sense of humour, and larger than life versions of an off the wall steampunk universe. Outside the exhibition centre, which was housed in a free standing large building, there was a coin operated steampunk engine with lights, engine and train noises, and spitting out fire and billows of smoke. Bill was in his element. Not really my thing, so I wandered off in the opposite direction and hoped I'd find my way back!
www.steampunkoamaru.co.nz

I eventually opted for a wander around the shops, all the time registering various buildings to memory, as I was liable to get totally lost, even in such a small town. I must say my navigational skills can be atrocious. I was hunting for wool and knitting needles, something to keep me busy in the evenings, as I was going to knit some gloves. What for you wonder? After all it was summer! You'll just have to wait and see. I also discovered Manuka honey, absolutely lovely. It's a mono-floral honey and is renowned for its antibacterial properties.

We met up again towards lunchtime, and as I walked towards Bill he had a sort of astonished look on his face. I knew what that was all about. "Don't look at me like that," I said, "sometimes Bill I do know where I am and where I'm going."

"Really?" was his only reply, I could feel one of my looks coming on. Oh yes!

Trotters Gorge and the Moeraki Boulders

We were eager to try one of the Department of conservation (DoC) sites, and as Trotters Gorge was on the way down to Dunedin we would stay there for one night. They were very cheap at about $6 (approx. £3.00) per person per night, but with few or no facilities. On the way to the Gorge we had decided to visit the Moeraki boulders, these were about 40 kilometres south of Oamaru but we wouldn't have too much time to spend there, as with my desperately need to improve navigational skills, it may have become difficult to find the smaller road to the Gorge. So, we negotiated, I would drive and Bill would navigate, it worked well. We reached the Moeraki boulders on Koekohe beach early in the afternoon, so we had plenty of time to have a good walk before we needed to be back on the road and on our way to Trotters Gorge.

The boulders are a group of large spherical stones, some almost two metres in diameter, they've a smooth surface with a honeycomb centre. They once lay deep in the mudstone cliffs behind the beach, and as the cliffs were eroded out fell the smooth boulders. Although according to Maori legend, they are from the wreckage of a legendary waka (canoe) and the boulders were the remains of eel

baskets, which had been washed up on the shoreline and turned into stone.
www.moerakiboulders.com

After a lovely stroll along the beach and a quick look in the gift shop we were back on State Highway 1 and heading west onto Horse Range Road in search of Trotters Gorge. On returning to the van we forgot about our previous arrangement, and somehow, I was navigating and Bill was driving, and with my wonderful sense of direction we seemed to pass the same place at least twice.

The van came to a sudden halt. Bill jumped out and said, "Drive!"

Er! What? I thought. "Ah, have we been circling?" I asked.

A grunt from Bill. "To say the least."

We were soon back on track again with me driving and Bill navigating. Oh, the joy of sharing our skills.

We eventually arrived at Trotters Gorge, a lovely peaceful place. It was in the bush and connected by two riverside tracks, basically a field by a stream in the middle of the bush with a toilet and a picnic bench, far away from the maddening crowds. Now that is an exaggeration as in New Zealand there are days you can drive for 100s of kilometres and not see a soul. We were warned about this before we left England. "Don't worry if you travel a good 100 or 200 kilometres and not see another vehicle it's just how it is," and how right they were. There was only one other camper van and one tent dweller arrived at the Gorge that night so it was very, very quiet, and very, very dark. In the morning, we had a peaceful breakfast and then walked up the gorge and climbed up through the bush and onto a rocky vantage point. It had wonderful views of big rock outcrops, and the two valleys leading from the gorge out to the sea.

We had to climb a large rock to see the panorama but I can't stand heights and I felt awfully dizzy as I heard Bill shouting from way above me.

"Come on up higher. Cor! Look at that view."

"Do I have to?" I replied

Dunedin

Dunedin was our next port of call. Dunedin is the second largest city on the South Island. I would call it the Scottish capital of New Zealand as it was founded by Scottish settlers. It houses New Zealand's first university, the University of Otago, and lies on the central eastern coast of Otago surrounding the Otago Harbour. The Otago gold rush occurred during the 1860s and it was one of New Zealand's biggest gold strikes. The gold rush spread throughout most of central Otago, which led to the rapid expansion, and commercialization of Dunedin, it grew quickly to become New Zealand's largest city at that time.

We were calling in here to stay with Bill's friends from York, Dorothy and Eli. What a lovely warm welcome we received, a much-appreciated meal, and a proper full size bed for the night. Wow! It doesn't get much better than that after a week or two in a small camper van!

On the Sunday, we went to Meeting for Worship and met with Dunedin Quakers. This included two Friends who had called to see us whilst we were still in Britain, to have a chat about New Zealand and the different Meetings. We stayed for tea and coffee and chatted to various people about our journey and the wonderful sites of the South Island. They were all anxious to know how people were coping in Christchurch, and so we related some stories to them, it was sad, but it was, after all, reality.

In the afternoon, Dorothy and Eli suggested we visit the Eco sanctuary at Orokonui, it was about 3.5 kilometres behind Port Chalmers and twenty minutes North of Dunedin. This centre houses some of New Zealand's rarest birds, reptiles, and plants in a protected forest setting. There was a range of walking tracks through the beautiful forest. It had taken less than ten years to make the only place on the South Island where native birds, animals and insects could live a life safe from predators. They were free to fly, feed, mate and nest wherever they wanted to and due to a large pest-proof project, a number of endangered species had been reintroduced.

Bill was very keen to see as many Birds of New Zealand as he possibly could, so this was probably the ideal place for him to see the tui, which so far had been very elusive.

It was a beautiful afternoon, and we were looking forward to a leisurely walk around the park, but when we arrived we noticed that the park closed at 4.30 p.m. Apparently, they would lock the gates even if you were still inside, so we didn't have as much time as we would have liked to have had. We made a quick decision as to which of the many paths we would take to see as much as possible. It was splendid listening to the bird's singing as we wandered around the forest, I say wandered, this excluded Bill. As ever, he was frantically chasing around looking for the tui bird. Yes, he can be quite animated and manic at times. Alas, thank goodness, the tui appeared and as usual where Bill least expected it to be. So, satisfied with our lovely afternoon we made our way to the exit just before they locked the gates, with a bit of joviality as to what would happen if we didn't make it in time.

As Bill was so intent on his tick list of birds, Dorothy and Eli encouraged us to listen out for "morepork," in the evenings. What on earth is "morepork?" It's an owl that instead of twit-ta-wooing, it says "morepork." I thought they were winding us up!

www.orokonui.org.nz

Eli then drove us to Port Chalmers. It was so lovely to be driven for a change by someone who knows where they're going, and without our usual banter and silences (of the Quaker kind of course).

Port Chalmers is a suburb of the main port of Dunedin arranged around cruise ship and shipping container berths, with a thriving creative arts community. Shipping containers have such diverse usage in New Zealand. It was also a port-of-call for several expeditions during the time of the Antarctica exploration. It was the last port visited by Captain Robert Falcon Scott, before he headed south on his final expedition to Antarctica. A large stone monument now stands above the town dedicated to Scott's expedition. We stood at this point and looked across the port to the outlying scenery with hilly mounds popping out of the sea. It was tranquil and refreshing.

Later that evening we stood in Eli and Dorothy's back garden listening for "morepork", but were our friends sat inside the house laughing, we did wonder?

Chapter 4

The Sound of the South

Monday, 28 November, and we had become aware that if we were to attend as many New Zealand Quaker meetings as possible, meet as many isolated Friends as we could, and to see as many of the wonderful sights of these intriguing islands, then we really had to motor on.

We hit the road again and he's singing that song,

"♪ Back on the road again da do de de da♪." I decided to ignore him this time and hope the song would go away. Even though it was becoming ever so annoying, totally out of tune and going downhill fast. Not the van, Bill!

We hadn't planned to do the whole journey to Milford Sound in one go and I had hoped we could stop off on the way, but Bill was keen to carry on and so the song continued. I promised myself I would get my own back, I just needed to wait, as timing would be essential.

Milford Sound was formed by the erosive effects of a glacier so could be classed more like a Norwegian Fjord. We drove down the coast to Balclutha and then across to Te Anau along the side of the lake and then up some 120 kilometres on the Milford Road to the Sound. It seemed a long way around but it's the only way and it was quite busy. Well, busy for a New Zealand road that is. The Homer tunnel, which is some 1270 metres long and was built between 1930 and 1954, cuts through the mountain range connecting the Hollyford River Valley to Milford Sound. As we journeyed the daylight was disappearing and darkness began to fall upon us. We eventually arrived at the mouth of the tunnel, but the traffic lights weren't working so we thought, oh well must be ok. The one camper van behind us just followed us through. We discovered the next day, that we had probably had a very near escape in the tunnel, as the traffic lights should have been on! I did say to Bill maybe they'd switched the lights off thinking everyone had arrived.

"Yer? Right Sil," was his sarcastic reply.

Sailing on Milford Sound

We hooked up at the camper park, which was very busy with people preparing to visit the Sound the next day, or having spent the day exploring it. It was a very serviceable graveled site with all the usual facilities as well as some cabins. Very practical, and it suited our purpose well.

The Maoris had discovered the Sound more than 1,000 years ago, and returned each year, via treks and pathways, to collect the precious 'pounamu' known as Greenstone or Jade. In 1912 John Grono was the first European settler to arrive at the Sound, he named it after Milford Haven in Wales. In no time at all others heard of the natural beauty of Milford Sound, and the writer Rudyard Kipling visited referring to it as the 'eighth wonder of the world'.

Off we set the next morning, with scarves, hats and raincoats, to book a cruise on the Milford Sound. It was a beautiful November morning, spring remember, although slightly chilly. The scenery was dramatic with steep cliffs, dense forests and snow topped mountains and at the highest point stood the Mitre Peak, some 1,692 metres above sea level. As waterfalls cascaded down the steep sides of the Sound, some were as high as 1,000 metres, we sailed out towards the Tasman Sea on what was described as a mixture of sea water and fresh water. On occasions, the water from the falls didn't actually reach the Sound, as it was blown back upwards and dispersed by the wind, or in the winter froze on the way down.

We were taken as close as was safely possible to the cliffs around the sides of the Sound, to see where the seals basked and black gulls were nesting. With its snow-topped mountains in the distance, this naturally magnificent sight could certainly be classed as the 'eighth wonder of the world'. Even though we were talking, the wildlife could still be heard along with the cascading waterfalls, and the gentle lapping of the water against the side of the boat. Yet, amazingly, there was still a sort of haunting, chilling silence in the air. Apparently, there are approximately 185 plus days of rain per year at Milford Sound, so we were repeatedly told how lucky we had been to have such a lovely sunny day. It's known to be the wettest area in New Zealand and probably the wettest in the world. Half way through the tour Bill spotted a pirate ship, and to the amusement of our fellow passengers gave a running commentary as to how we would chase them back out to sea.

"Ahoy," he said, "go on you beggars we've got you now," and so he continued. Unfortunately, I had nowhere to hide. Give me the man and I'll show you the boy!

On the way-back there was a salmon fish farm station, where some people alighted, but we hadn't planned this stop off as we were becoming ever more conscious of our schedule. Ok, my schedule. Well, what a wonderful mornings sail, and the weather had been so kind, we felt truly exhilarated.

After our sail on Milford Sound we were to make our way to Te Anau, hopefully to arrive later in the afternoon. A wave goodbye to the Sound and of course the lovely boat crew, and we climbed back into our ever-faithful Isaacs' van, who had kept his plumbing in check all the way! But then I couldn't believe it. Not again! This was becoming tiresome, Bill was singing that song,

"We're on the road again, do de da da do," and it was getting worse, as this time he was well out of tune and the "do da dos," where he didn't know the words were awful. How on earth could I concentrate to drive. 'Canned Heat' you have a lot to answer for!

Ah, at last it came to me. As soon as Bill stopped singing I serenaded him with, "The hills are alive with the sound of Milford," oh boy did I exaggerate my "do de, do das."

I can't actually explain the look he gave me. I didn't sing for long though, I couldn't, because I just went into fits of laughter at the look on his face.

It was a much slower journey out of the Sound, than our hasty dash the night before, as we pulled up to take photographs at every opportunity we could. As we'd assumed there wouldn't be time to travel this way again. We were amazed to see masses of lupins growing along the roadside, and in the wide pebble filled courses of the rivers. Their colours were vibrant and powerful, with pinks, purples, blues, oranges and yellows, swaying magnificently in the morning sunlight. We admired these English Country garden flowers only to be told that they're classed as a 'noxious weed' in New Zealand. They were apparently introduced in the 1950s by a farmer's wife, who longed for more colour along the roadsides. Wow! Wish we had some noxious weeds like those in our back garden.

On the way down, after passing over the highest point, we found a place for a short walk called the 'Chasm'. It was a water sculptured rock gorge. There was a car park and a short walk through the forest over footbridges to the Chasm. Thousands of years of gushing water had sculpted shapes into the rocks with some dramatic effects, and guess who we met there? You wouldn't believe it, one of the rocks looked like 'ET' from the movie. (See Bill and Sil's Amazing New Zealand Adventure blog.)

Whilst parked at the 'Chasm' we would take a break for lunch, or as we had started to call it, 'time to raid the fridge.' It was a very peaceful place and really quiet, in fact not busy at all. Bill parked right next to the only other vehicle in the quite large car park, where there was a young family also enjoying their lunch stop. I had hoped to have a nice secluded lunch. However, this wasn't going to happen with the busy little family next to us. After an exchange of words with Bill, you know what I mean, he moved the van over to a corner where we could relax, and have a bite to eat, a mug of tea and a read of our books.

Tin of tuna open (big mistake), salad and bread rolls at the ready, we put the chairs to the side of the van and settled down for a half hour or so of pleasure. In no time at all three kea birds appeared, and began to dance around us and tried their best to jump onto our laps, and help us enjoy our food. We had just got comfy again, after a bit of determined effort to ignore them and salvage our lunch break, when we heard a bit of a racket and a lot of excited talking. We looked up to see that a coach had arrived. Japanese tourists were jumping off the bus and running towards us, cameras at the ready and it was click, click of their cameras as they surrounded poor Isaac taking pictures of those cheeky birds. Great, privacy completely shattered! What I had thought would be a nice quiet lunch break had turned into a bit of a circus.

We just looked up, smiled and said, "Cheese."

Now, if anyone from Japan shows you their holiday snaps of New Zealand, you may see a very small camper van, with two people sat on chairs, silly grins on their faces, eating lunch whilst the kea parrots dance around them for any little scraps they could scavenge.

The kea parrot is about 19 inches long, has olive green plumage and is mainly found in the forested and Alpine regions of the South Island. It's the world's only Alpine parrot. They are known for their curiosity and intelligence. Apparently, they can solve logical puzzles and push or pull things to obtain food. There are signs in a lot of car parks and campsites asking you not to feed the kea parrot. They are also known as the 'Clown of the Mountains' and are just as likely to chew your shoes, rucksacks or anything with rubber or leather, or even carry off small unguarded items.

Believe us we've seen them. Oh, how they can work it!

Lake Te Anau

After our eventful lunch, we headed on to Lake Te Anau to hook up overnight. It was a beautiful drive along the side of the lake, which held the reflection of the snow-topped mountains, as the sun sparkled on the blue water. We were to stay at the Lake Te Anau Holiday park, which was beside the lake and only a few minutes' walk from the town.

Lake Te Anau is one of New Zealand's biggest and deepest lakes with the hillsides covered with dense forest. It's classed as the gateway town to Fiordland. Although, we'd travelled the opposite way around and were using the park as a one night stop over on the way back. It's a very small town with a population of about 1,500 and not a lot happening, but that doesn't matter because Lake Te Anau has enough to offer with its beautiful scenery. It can also be the starting point of some tramps, one of the most popular being the Milford Track which starts just across the lake.

'Tramp' – not a scruffy unshaven old man, but a Kiwi word for a walk in the forests, hills and mountains.

We spent a leisurely evening at Lake Te Anau, had a good meal and a restful night's sleep, then in the morning we did our usual routine and hit the road again. Not too far from Lake Te Anau, we felt compelled to stop at Manapouri, a small delightful community, with very little except houses and a lake, Lake Manapouri. It was quite isolated, and we enjoyed a lovely stroll along the walkways and a quick cup of tea. This was one of the pluses of our wee camper van, we could brew up at any time, as long as one of us had remembered to fill the water tank! There was something mystical about walking alongside the lake, with the water shimmering in the sunshine and gently lapping against the shore. After our dash up to Milford Sound, it seemed fitting to enjoy the silence and the beauty of nature in this fairly isolated area. Oh, how silence can be golden, it can refresh the body and the soul. Back to reality and on the road again, and he hadn't sung since my wonderful rendition of, 'The hills are alive with the sound of Milford.' Wow, I thought I've put an end to his "do do das."

Invercargill

Feeling refreshed, we pushed on to the southernmost point on the South Island, Invercargill. We hadn't planned where to stay in the Invercargill area so after an hour or so touring around, and we were both becoming quite tetchy, hot and hungry or maybe hungry, hot and tetchy. Who knows? A quick decision was made, we'd head out of the town and see what we might fall upon, and there it was, a lovely site a few kilometers outside Invercargill on Dunns Road, Otatara, the Beach Road Holiday Park at Sandy Point. This holiday park was close to Oreti Beach and was set in six hectares of mature, sheltered parkland. It was a short walk to the nearest bar/tavern, which we visited and enjoyed the natural beauty of this area along with a welcome glass of beer. We felt quite comfortable here and there were plenty of walking tracks so we stayed a couple of nights. This enabled us to catch up on a big wash, clothes not ourselves, and write up some more of the blog, 'Bill and Sil's Amazing New Zealand Adventure.'

Invercargill is the most southern and western city in New Zealand, and one of the most southern cities in the world. It is classed as the commercial centre of the Southland Region. Many of the streets in the centre of the city are named after British rivers, Forth, Tyne, Esk, Thames, Don and Mersey to name but a few.

Settled in the mid 1850s Southland saw an early-extended contact between Europeans and Maori, with sealers, whalers and missionaries arriving. In 1853 Walter Mantell purchased Murihiku from a local Maori, Iwi, claiming the land for European settlement. Otago, which Southland was part of, was the subject of planned settlement by the Free Church, an off-shoot of the Presbyterian Church of Scotland. Due to the Otago gold rush the population grew in the 1860s. The major growth today is the increased demand for New Zealand milk, cheese and butter. New Dairy factories had opened and it was also the home of the Southern Institute of Technology, which had introduced a zero fees scheme, this had helped to rejuvenate the city.

We attended a Meeting for Worship with a house group in Invercargill on the Thursday evening. We were made to feel very welcome, and it was lovely to chat with the group while having some light refreshments. We found it amazing, how interested people were when they discovered why we were touring New Zealand. Lots of Kiwis said, "Wow six months, that's cool."

The house group was a lovely small part of the community, and the lady who hosted the group even had a good sized Quaker sign in her front garden. They were lovely people, who enjoyed their Thursday evenings together to worship, but also to catch up with each other's lives. They were anxious to hear our news of Christchurch, so we divulged as much as we thought was necessary, being ever thoughtful, as no one knows when or where the next earthquake may strike. New Zealand is well known for its volcanic and earthquake activity, due to its position next to the Australian and Pacific plates.

We said our farewells and wished our Invercargill Friends love, light and peace. The next morning, we were up bright and early, all jobs done and on the road back up to Dunedin.

Otago Peninsula

It was Friday, 2 December and we were back in Dunedin. We arrived at Dorothy and Eli's to yet another warm welcome, a lovely meal and a full-sized bed. We were as ever, so very grateful for this.

On the Saturday morning, there was to be quite a large farmers market in Dunedin, so we spent a couple of hours wandering around, looking at all the delightful foods on offer. We couldn't be tempted though, as our fridge wouldn't take the strain, but when we saw all the delicious fresh food it would have been so easy to buy, buy, buy!

We both reminded each other.

"No! No fridge space! Waste!"

In the afternoon, we were to give our first presentation of the Quaker story to the Dunedin Meeting. Before we'd left Britain, we'd worked very hard on a project to take the story of early Quaker beginnings in Britain to New Zealand. We searched for pictures, photographs and sketches to try and bring to life the experience as best we could. Eventually, with the help of a friend, who was passionate about history, we had a very presentable power point presentation, and of course with the ever-enthusiastic Bill as presenter, what could possibly go wrong? Having had a couple of quick, dry runs at home, we both realized that at times I had to guide Bill back to the story. Reminding him where he was in the telling of the tale, as off on a tangent he would go, which was usually quite interesting but could lead to a path far from the story!

When he realized, he'd lost the plot, he'd look at me, like a little lost school boy, and say, "Where was I?"

Oh and of course, if Bill had had free rein on the presentation it would have taken hours, and hours, everyone would be snoozing or trying very hard to look interested. His time keeping could be quite hard to control, as he would deliberately avoid looking in my direction, except when he had lost his way. Yes, he knew to keep his eyes off mine or I would be tapping my watch, although, we usually got there in the end. Dunedin Friends response was good so we were very pleased, some said it had filled gaps for them in their knowledge of Quaker history.

Later in the afternoon we were invited by two Friends from Dunedin Meeting, to go for a drive, a late picnic lunch, and some sightseeing. We were driven out onto the Otago Peninsula, which divides the Otago Harbour from the Pacific Ocean, and stopped at one of the many little bays to have lunch. It was a real treat once again, enjoying food that someone else had prepared, and taking in the sights and sounds of natural New Zealand.

After lunch, we packed up and drove around the winding bay watching for wildlife, as our guides recounted some of the history of the area. We were eventually heading for the Royal Albatross Centre at Taiaroa Head, a protected area where several colonies of sea mammals and sea birds congregate. It's apparently the only mainland colony of albatross in the world. In the Information Centre, there were galleries with interesting information and views of wildlife, as well as the history of the area, along with a café. Outside there were lots of gulls nesting with their chicks. The gulls would fly off and their young would make the most ear-piercing noise as they squawked and screeched, and cawed for their parents to return with more food. There were literally hundreds of them. They were everywhere. We discovered we were too early to see the albatross arrive back to their nests, so made the decision to return later.

It was about 4 o'clock in the afternoon, so we drove back down the winding road to visit the Otakou Marae, which is a fenced complex of buildings and grounds for the local Maori tribes. The Marae refers to the entire complex, a base for the community, with a Meeting House, Church and burial ground. It was a place for celebrations, functions, political meetings and religious/spiritual gatherings. We spent a pleasant hour or so at the Marae Meeting House, wandering around the grounds, admiring the red Maori carvings on the buildings, and looking at the different plants and grasses, before we returned to the Albatross Centre.

It was 5.45 p.m. and we hoped we weren't too late to see the albatross return. No disappointment this time though. Oh, boy did we get a spectacular fly-by. As soon as we had alighted from the car, Bill marched off towards the cliff edge, to where the gulls were nesting. Binoculars as usual slung over his shoulder, and with a steely determination to see the royal albatross, he strode off ahead of us. Some people were beginning to leave the site, obviously disappointed, at not having seen the royal albatross. As Bill was wandering around, binoculars glued to his eyes, and looking skywards this huge bird effortlessly glided over his head.

"Bill put your binoculars down and look directly above you," I yelled at him.

It was a sight of splendid gliding magnificence.

"Why?" Bill shouted back,

"Erm! You might like what you see," I said rather nonchalantly.

He gave me one of those, 'I'll just appease her,' looks and looked up. Well, you could have knocked him over with a feather, he couldn't believe it. He dropped his binoculars and just stood in awe, as the albatross glided, ever so smoothly, about 4 metres above his head. He then went ape, with surprise and delight. Not a pretty sight! There they were, the royal albatross, coming home to nest. People started to run back to where we were stood.

"Look, look, look," a very excited Bill was yelling. It was just too incredible to describe and certainly had to be seen to be believed.

The royal albatross with its 3.3 metre wing span was a graceful and elegant spectacle gliding along majestically, whereas the gulls were flapping and squawking like mad and even trying to dive bomb the albatross. It's one of the world's largest birds, and has been the subject of reverence and superstition. The Maori legend says that it is the embodiment of a dead sea captain's soul condemned to drift the oceans forever. I must say, they look very peaceful though. They're solitary creatures and spend most of their life on the wing or at sea.

www.albatross.org.nz

Job done, box ticked, as Bill would say. So off back to Dorothy and Eli's, where they were preparing a lovely fish supper for the six of us.

The next day was Sunday, 4 December and it was warm and sunny, it felt strange that it was getting warmer in December, instead of cooler. We went to Meeting for Worship at Dunedin Meeting House and afterwards led the Meeting in a session on the Quaker Testimonies. Again, it was a very well received session with lots of discussion and points being raised.

It was soon Monday morning and we were heading northbound, so with goodbyes, hugs, misty eyes and a promise to try to squeeze in another visit we were back on State Highway 1.

I was so disappointed as Bill had started to sing, "We're on the road again."

He'd obviously forgotten that two can play this game. Although what was he up to, I wondered, as he had a bit of a smirk on his face. Mmm, worrying! Then I realised he knew it annoyed me.

On the way back up to Christchurch, we booked into the Kelceys' Bush Farmyard Holiday Park near Waimate, for a one-night stopover. Nestling in the Hunter Hills it was a unique park with nature at its best. Definitely a family holiday park with play areas, a farmyard animal park, bush walks, – a discover wallabies after dusk safari, as well as native flora and fauna. We thought we'd go on the 'discover the wallabies trail' and as it had started to rain we put on all the usual clobber, kagouls, boots, waterproof over trousers etc. Then as we stood looking at each other, outside the van, and with the rain trickling down our faces Bill said, "What are we doing? We're the only wallabies daft enough to be out in the rain tonight, let's give it a miss."

I didn't need much encouragement, so off with our rain attire and back into the van. We were all snug and warm in our little tin tent on wheels and fell asleep to the sound of the rain pitter pattering on the roof.

We awoke the next morning to glorious sunshine peeping through the curtains, and the sound of the bellbird and tui serenading us. We were up with the larks. No! The bellbird and the tui. Oh, country life, it was a joy to hear the sounds of the natural environment. Chores done and we were driving back up to Christchurch from Waimate. The scenery was fantastic with long bridges crossing the winding rivers. We pulled off the highway for tea and a nibble, (not many kilometres pass before Bill must have his cuppa), at Timaru ex railway station café. It seemed to be a very popular meeting place and would probably have been a very busy station pre-1960s. Beeching's equivalent did a big cutting job of the railways and most of New Zealand rail was now only freight, although the TranzAlpine line (see later) was available to passengers, mainly tourists. There were seven coal trains a day helping pay for its upkeep, very good low ash coal was being exported from Alpine mines to Asia and India for steel making.

Chapter 5

Earthquake News

We arrived back in Christchurch and checked into our favorite site Amber Park. We later attended the Christchurch Quaker Monthly Meeting, where the Threshing Meeting Minute was accepted and two groups were set up to move the Meeting forward. This was excellent news, we were really delighted for all involved. There was a big sigh of relief from the members of the Meeting, as this had been one of the hurdles that had been challenging them. It also meant at last they could begin to plan for the future of the Meeting.

On our last visit to Christchurch we'd discovered the small suburb of Riccarton, with a shopping centre, restaurants, cinema etc., it was also quite a handy distance from Amber Park. We were shopping there and I had a chat with two young women about the effects the earthquakes and tremors were having on their lives. They told me a lot of people wouldn't go into the shopping mall anymore, for fear of it collapsing if there was another big one.

One of the young women told me of a friend, who had been in touch with a family from another country and had become very good friends with their daughter. She'd spent months persuading the girl's parents to allow their daughter to study English in New Zealand, re-assuring them that New Zealand was probably one of the safest countries in the world. The girl arrived in Christchurch to attend the language school, but within four days of her having arrived, the big one struck and she died along with many others. The young women's friend felt totally responsible, and was carrying some of the blame. She couldn't come to terms with it and the situation was having a snowball effect on the people around her. How do you deal with something like that?

The other young woman I spoke to had just got to know a young couple with a little boy. They had set up a business and were very happy. As another big earthquake struck they lost the building, but much, much worse, they lost their little boy. Shattered people were all around this community, but still they strove on to repair and rebuild their lives.

When a City Falls

That evening we went to the cinema to see the film "When a City Falls", a documentary about the earthquakes and tremors in Christchurch. There was another big one whilst they were shooting the film and the footage is just incredible and frightening. I don't think there was a dry eye in the cinema. It was so emotional. It revealed the true horror and devastation the earthquakes were having on the city and the people.

From the write up of the film: 'When a City Falls'
Filmmaker Gerard Smythe, said,
"He could never have planned to make a movie like this."
"Spring, 2010 and all is well on the Canterbury Plains. Lambs, blue skies and daffodils. Punts push new season's tourist along Christchurch's Avon River. They photograph the 'Garden City' the 'most English City outside of England'. We get hit with a 7.1 earthquake. We stand up, wave our fists at the heavens and compliment ourselves on our ability to recover.

And then we get hit even harder. Now the city has fallen. Many are dead. Many injured. Many narrowly escape.

A fragile people reappear in the following days. Once again, a response is growing. Communities are rising from the sand. People are holding tight. And now the whole country is rallying for Christchurch."

'When a city falls travels beyond earthquake reactive television footage to a tale of hope, to an inspiring observation of the kindness of human hearts.'

My account of the movie 'When a City Falls'
'The film is an in depth look at the damage and destruction in Christchurch after the first earthquake, but whilst filming in the city, another big earthquake struck. There are violent rumbles; the sound

of glass breaking; the piercing noise of car and security alarms all around, whilst the earthquake continued to take its toll.

There are smashed cars with bricks and cement on them. People are in shock! Some are stood still in the street, dazed, looking around them whilst others are running and screaming and crying.

Water is seeping up into the road and now to add to the noise there are police, ambulance and fire services sirens. All the emergency services are stretched beyond belief.

As the aftershocks continue to roll, a group of students gather together, organized on Facebook, to help clear some of the liquefaction.

One lady stated, "I'm not on my own, there are people out there who care."

There's no water; no working sewage system; no power; no 'phones.

The aftershocks rumble on as they continue to film.

Cranes move in and houses and other buildings are being demolished. Some had no insurance. Others were paying a mortgage on a house they could no longer live in. But no lives were lost.

And then came the next big one in February, 2011.

People are screaming, car alarms and sirens can be heard amidst the roaring and rumbling of the earthquake. Panic sets in, as the aftershocks continue one after another.

There's chaos as workers try to vacate the offices and shops. Some crawling out, others trapped in cars and buildings. People were being asked to leave the city. Some are trying to find or contact their loved ones. They're all being asked to leave and make way for the emergency services. The aftershocks continue. The top of the cathedral lies on the pavement. Helicopters can be heard overhead, circling and circling.

Then the biggest devastation of all, was that of the dead and the injured being carried out of the buildings, pulled from cars, and other vehicles. Eventually the buildings and the streets are empty, except for abandoned cars and the emergency services. Lives are shattered.

And the aftershocks continue! This was a state of emergency.'
www.whenacityfalls.co.nz   www.frankfilm.co.nz

'We had an earthquake at my school. I was really brave. I was eating lunch and I heard a noise. Everything was starting to shake. All our news fell off the teachers writing board. We did 'turtle safe' under our desks. John and me were under our desk. Mandy was on her own under her desk. Anne and Trevor were outside. My teacher had gone to eat lunch. She came back and we held hands and went onto the grass. Some of the children were so scared they began to cry. Mummy took a long time to come and pick me up. There were more little earthquakes all night. I slept under mummy's desk. Our home is ok. My photo fell down and things fell off the bookshelf. Some things got broken and mummy had to throw them in the rubbish. I don't like earthquakes'.

Adapted from a Friends Newsletter

The after-shocks continued in Christchurch and the surrounding areas. More and more buildings were being given a 'red zone' status and were being prepared for demolition. We travelled yet again into the city centre and could see that it was by no means over, this once wonderful city was under gradual demolition with buildings disappearing day by day.

Colour-coded zones
Colour-coded zones had appeared throughout the city.
Red Zone: Extensive damage to property and buildings. At risk of further damage from aftershocks. Due for demolition. No public access.
Orange Zone: Further assessment needed. Uncertain state of infrastructure. Will eventually be red zoned or green zoned.
Green Zone: Due for repair or re-build.
White Zone: Unassessed land

The people of Christchurch were being tested, their reserves at an all-time low. Christchurch cathedral was in ruins. Buckled and twisted roads, gnarled buildings, roofless homes, broken windows and broken hearts. The only apparent movement seemed to be the red zone which was becoming bigger and bigger. Demolition was moving at a faster pace. Insurance companies weren't paying out for re-builds until a relevant time of cessation of seismic activity, which could take years.

Familiar land marks had disappeared. People were leaving their homes and businesses and looking for alternative accommodation. Some left the city.

We felt helpless and bemused. We could hear their crying hearts, but all we had been able to do was listen and have compassion. We were soon to move on and leave this devastated city behind, but it and its people would be in our thoughts and our prayers. We promised we would be back.

Chapter 6

Northwards Bound via Whale Watching Seas

TranzAlpine Train Journey
Two Friends from Christchurch Meeting offered us a bed for a couple of nights at their home in the Paranui district of Christchurch, and we gratefully accepted. We were due to leave the city in a couple of days' time, to travel up the South Island and eventually sail to the North Island. Bill had talked about the TranzAlpine train excursion and so we decided to use this time to fulfil his passion for locomotives. Oh dear, I did occasionally indulge him. We parked the camper van on their drive and were made to feel very welcome in their lovely home. Ah, it was heaven not to have to pull the table down and make the bed up. Oh yes, and wrestle over the two duvets.

We had an early start the next morning, as we were to join the TranzAlpine train from Christchurch to Greymouth, some 223 kilometres each way. It's said to be one of the world's great train journeys with spectacular scenery and views. We arrived at the station early, yes me again, just in case we miss the train, by this time Bill was becoming quite amused by my 'need to be early.' Bill was very excited, as he loves train journeys, especially ones with high expectations such as this one. I just hoped he wouldn't be disappointed.

The train arrived and Bill disappeared onto the first carriage, I could hardly keep up with him. There was a good commentary both ways, plus we bought a couple of pictorial text guidebooks to peruse along the journey. It had a really good open-air viewing carriage, although on the way to Arthur's Pass it was very crowded and allowed for elbowroom only. That is to say, you needed to have your elbows out and hang on to get some good shots.

There was a rather large group of Japanese tourists and yes, they were as 'snap happy' as usual, so we had to squeeze through them to get any shots. Had we known they would be alighting before the end of the journey, we'd have saved ourselves the hassle and waited until they had done so. As soon as they'd left the train we shot back to the viewing carriage to watch the spectacular countryside roll by. Although there will always be someone, who will try and tell you how you should be doing something! A very, not so helpful guy, with the same camera as mine repeatedly told me I was holding it wrong, or I should be doing this, or that. It was ever so annoying as he followed me from carriage to carriage, and told me 'HE' was an expert. Oh dear, only one way to deal with him. He got one of my looks as I went off into my own little world and completely ignored him. I can hear him now in the background, with his Scandinavian accent going on and on about the camera. Arghhhhhh! Shut Up!

There were lots of trestle bridges over gorges and chasms, and multi course rivers running out from the mountains. The colour of the water was ever changing, from turquoises to blues to greens, as we sped around bends and along hillsides. My new camera, once I was left to get on with it, with its powerful lens, came into its own as I snapped views that shot before our eyes and then disappeared behind trees or as we entered a tunnel. There were 19 tunnels, the longest being 8.5 kilometres. It was wonderful scenery, with landscapes that told stories of the history of the early settlers' desire to get through the alps one way or another. The train came to a halt at Arthur's pass with its beech forest, mountain views and merino sheep station, where we alighted to stretch our legs.

Arthur's Pass and township were named after Sir Arthur Dudley Dobson. Thomas Cass, the Chief Surveyor, had asked him to find out if there was a route through the Waimakariri watershed into the valleys running to the west coast. In 1864, Arthur, joined by his brother, Edward, went into the valley of the Otira River. A west coast Maori Chief, Tarapuhi, told Arthur that there was a pass that Maori hunters used. Arthur returned to Christchurch and drew a map of the area marking the routes and sent it along with a report to Cass. Arthur named the pass site Camping Flat. When the gold rush began, some business men offered a prize of £200, for anyone who could find a better route from Canterbury to the west coast. At the same time Edward Dobson, Arthur's father, was sent to examine the passes and he reported back that "Arthur's" pass was the most suitable for direct crossing. The township then re-named Bealey Flats, after the second Superintendent Samuel Bealey, was originally built as a construction village for the building of the Otira tunnel which was started in 1908. The construction of the tunnel was very slow and it was eventually completed in 1923.

We arrived in Greymouth at approximately 12.45 p.m. with an hour or so to have a wander around, and have a bite to eat. This is the largest town on the west coast, another gold rush town in the early days. The Grey River pushes through over the treacherous sand bar to the sea. There had been devastating floods in Greymouth, when the river had burst its banks in the winter months, but as it was summer it lay calm and languid.

We were fascinated when we saw a homemade car parked on the street, it reminded us of 'Steampunk'. We were busy making funny noises and sort of pretending to drive off in it, with a real 'vroom vroom', you know just like children do. Can you imagine how surprised we were, when we turned around to see this chap smirking at us! I'm quite sure he was having a problem holding his mirth. It would appear he was the owner of the vehicle, so we made lots of polite noises like oohs and aahs, and asked could we take a picture, to which he agreed, and then he wandered off shaking his head.

We hurried back to the train station for our return journey to Christchurch. The train was much quieter on the way back so we had lots of opportunities for photographs, without someone telling me how to use my camera. It was also lovely just sitting there in the peace and quiet, as we watched the countryside roll by.

We arrived back in Christchurch just after 6 p.m. and made our way back to Paranui after a truly superb experience on the TranzAlpine train.

www.tranzscenic.co.nz

Kaikoura

We left Paranui with many thanks to our hosts for their hospitality, and two very restful nights, and continued our onward journey up the South Island to Kaikoura. With sadness, we were saying goodbye to Christchurch until the following year, even with its rubble and problems, we had become quite attached to the people and the city. We were heading northwards up the east coast of the South Island to catch the Ferry to the North Island, where we would continue our travels and Meetings. We drove up State Highway 1 from Christchurch, through mainly farmland to begin with, and later on to winding roads, passing a rocky coastline on the one side and hills and mountains on the other. It was a pleasant and uneventful journey of some 185 kilometres to reach Kaikoura and Bill didn't sing. Phew. What a relief!

We arrived in Kaikoura mid-afternoon and soon found the Top 10 Holiday Park on Beach Road, it was a lovely park, with amazing mountain views and quite near the town.

Kaikoura is set on a peninsula between the slightly snow topped mountains of the Seaward Kaikoura Range and the Pacific Ocean. This was the place to whale watch or swim with dolphins, the seabed drops rapidly and so encourages large sea mammals to feed nearer the shores. It was a small, but quite picturesque town, with a sort of a 'wild west' feel about the main street and the buildings.

The name Kaikoura came about when an ancient Maori explorer stopped to eat crayfish, and found it so good that he named the place KAI meaning food, and KOURA meaning crayfish. The first Europeans to settle in the area were whalers in the early 1840s and were soon followed by farmers. Kaikoura earned its place on the tourist map in the late 1980s as 'whale watching' and 'swimming with dolphins' became more popular. It was expanding, becoming more commercial but it hadn't lost its small town, South Island feel.

We'd been told of a lady who was an attender at Marlborough Meeting, but for several reasons had been unable to attend a Meeting for Worship for some time, also due to the distance from Kaikoura to Marlborough. We gave her a call and asked if she would like to meet up. She occasionally played the organ in the Presbyterian Church, so we would attend the morning service on Sunday, to meet with her afterwards. It was a lovely service and everyone made us feel very welcome. After this we had a cup of tea and some fresh cherries, which the minister had provided, absolutely yummy! The minister said it would be ok for us to have a half an hour Meeting for Worship with our friend in the church, as he commented, "You are after all a Christian group."

It was good to be able to do this as she had wanted to chat as well and didn't see many Quakers. She seemed to be fairly Quaker isolated and missed the silent worship. We met up with her once again that evening at the Ecumenical Carol Service in the local Anglican Church. Walking to a carol service in the evening in full sunshine played silly games with our brains, it was quite weird. Both the churches were lovely warm wood finished buildings, unlike the dark stone ones we tend to have in the United Kingdom. The carol service was really uplifting, especially on this light and sunny evening, and it did make us both think of our families preparing for Christmas. I had become slightly home sick by this time as Christmas without family seemed an onerous task. The locals were very friendly and plied us with tea and snacks. We even got an invite to someone's home for lunch the next day, but amongst it all we didn't get the directions properly and had one of our little differences!

"No, he said this way, no he said that way, no, no, no, you got it wrong," you know how it goes, navigator versus driver.

Then I said, "Did you get his number or address?"

We just looked at each other in dismay as we hadn't even got his name. Maybe he was just being polite! What a shame because he was a lovely, interesting chap. Anyway, this nice man had made sure we got a couple of copies of the carols, so we could sing them the following year at home.

Carol Our Christmas

Carol our Christmas an upside-down Christmas;
Snow is not falling and trees are not bare.
Carol the summer, and welcome the Christ Child,
Warm in our sunshine and sweetness of air.

Sing of the gold and the green and the sparkle,
Water and river and lure of the beach.
Sing in the happiness of open spaces,
Sing a nativity summer can reach.

Shepherds and Musterers over hillsides,
Finding not angels but sheep to be shorn;
Wise ones make journeys whatever the season,
Searching for signs of the truth to be born.

Right side up Christmas belongs to the universe,
Made in the moment a woman gives birth;
Hope is the Jesus gift, love is the offering,
everywhere, anywhere here on the earth.

(words and music by Shirley Erena Murray and Colin Gibson)

On the Monday Bill went for a walk into Kaikoura, whilst I caught up with correspondence, blog writing and of course the usual tidying of the van and washing chores. Later in the afternoon a very excited Bill arrived back at the van.

"I've got something fantastic for you for your Christmas present," he enthused.

I smiled to myself and thought, well the carol service has definitely gone to his head it's only 12 December and he's started Christmas shopping. Wow! This was a first. Yet, I really didn't know where this was going.

"Oh lovely," I said, "that's nice."

"Here you can have it now," Bill said with a big grin on his face.

"No, no – Christmas Day will do thank you, I don't want to spoil your surprise," I replied.

"Oh no, you must have it today," he said placing an envelope in my hand.

Erm! This was becoming worrying he was just too excited, which could only have meant that Bill would enjoy the surprise too!

"Bill I don't want it now, I'd rather wait until Christmas," I retorted beginning to get fed up with Christmas already.

"Sylvia, it's not an option we're doing it tomorrow."

Ahh! Now this made me nervous.

"Doing it tomorrow?" I repeated. I could feel the panic rising in my stomach.

"Yes, yes, open it, it's wonderful, I'm so excited," Bill was leaping around, yes, he does leap around when he's excited.

Mmmm, I thought, you're excited but will I be?

Carefully opening the envelope, you never know with Bill what might pop out. I stared at two tickets and said in a voice that even I didn't recognize. "Whale watching, are you kidding, whale watching for Christmas, not a chance."

After a strong discussion, of many words, I succumbed but not for Christmas. We would go whale watching the next day, but no way for my Christmas present.

Kaikoura is home to New Zealand's main population of sperm whales. Apparently, there is nowhere else in the world that this species is routinely found so close to the coast. They congregate here because of the 3 kilometres deep Kaikoura Canyon running up against the coast, creates a rare system of sea currents, that sustain an incredibly rich marine food chain. They can be up to 18.5 metres long and weigh 57 tons and there can be about 85 sperm whales in this area. The sperm whale was one of the most heavily exploited sea mammals during the whale hunting times.

I awoke early the next morning to the joys of Bill singing and a big mug of tea thrust into my hand.

"Come on, rise and shine, big day today. Oh sorry, I mean big whale day today. Happy Christmas," Bill said with that silly grin on his face.

Calm, I thought, just stay calm. It was very difficult indeed.

Off we trotted, Bill marched on in front, a large mug of tea in one hand and the tickets in his other hand. I suggested that maybe the mug of tea wasn't such a good idea, as it was his fourth that morning and he may feel queasy. He insisted he would be fine, as he had his travel sickness bands in his pocket and would put them on before embarking onto the boat. I didn't know whether I would be fine though! Whale watching just wasn't my sort of thing, especially not for Christmas!

We arrived at the Whale Watching Centre in good time. Bill flashed the tickets at a young woman behind the reception desk and said, "Christmas present."

She looked puzzled. She then realized it would be better to ignore the comment as I shook my head and walked away. As soon as we had checked in and been given details of what would happen next, Bill decided I should have some travel bands too, because I was sure to be sea sick.

"After all," he said, "you can't even look over the side of a mountain without going dizzy and feeling sick."

Ok Bill, point taken.

"There we go," Bill produced a rather nice looking pair of blue travel sickness bands, "another Christmas present for you."

I think that was the point when I nearly lost the plot, but decided it was just a bit too public. Oh well, every dog has its day so they say. Bill was still fussing about my bands being in the right place on my wrists as we boarded the catamaran and were ready for the off. We were told to make our way to a seat below deck as quickly as possible and to remain seated until the crew spotted any whales. They would then instruct us as to when we could leave our seats and go up onto the top viewing deck. As we left the harbour the sea was very choppy, so I thought that maybe the extra Christmas present from Bill would come in handy after all. We sped along the water as we fleetingly passed the green countryside and left the town behind. We were given all the safety instructions including dealing with seasickness as they said, "We're used to it, as there's always one!"

The catamaran came to a sudden halt. A whale had been spotted, so we were allowed to go up onto the top deck to view this incredible mammal. I couldn't believe the size of this huge, shiny, black whale just lolling on top of the water. They do this to take in oxygen before they dive with a flip of their tail and carry on with their journey. The body of the whale was big enough to step onto, not that we did, like an enormous stage and so solid looking. Apparently, this whale is usually there at about the same time each day, so the crew could just about guarantee a viewing. As we stood on the top deck the whale showed no sign of flipping its tail for us and going off to sea. The crew then spotted another whale some way away. So off we set at speed, bouncing up and down on the waves, hanging on to the rails. But when I turned and looked at Bill, he was looking a little pale and perspiring.

"You ok?" I asked

"Yes, yes, I just want to see the next whale," replied Bill with a now sallow green look to his gills!

It was a little chilly and quite windy out on the Pacific Ocean but the crew soon found the next whale, which they reckoned was just about to flip its tail. I took a quick glance Bill's way, who by now truly was becoming the Greenman. You see he also always wears green, yes, I know, weird! I then turned to steady my camera and focus on the whale, what a shot it was going to be with my new camera. By the time, I'd focused and went to shoot, there was nothing there, gone, missed it! I couldn't believe it. Maybe I should have listened to the little man on the TranzAlpine train after all!

"What…..? Where's it gone?" I said, astounded that I'd missed what could probably have been one of the best shots I would ever take. Bill and the other passengers couldn't contain themselves, they were raving at the sight they'd just witnessed.

"Wow, Wow, immense did you see that," as they were pointing to the sea.

"Sil. Sil did you get it?" Bill was yelling

"Bill, Bill, no!" I yelled back above the noise of the catamaran and the ocean. Bill thought it was really funny that I'd missed it completely, and laughed almost hysterically.

Then we were off again, the catamaran bounced over the waves as we went back to the first whale. We had to hold our places next to the rails, as everyone was trying to get the best view possible. I was struggling to get back into position as some people seemed to have managed to push in front of me. I think I was too busy trying to make sure my camera was set properly for the next shot. However, this was soon resolved, as Bill couldn't contain himself any longer. Oh dear! He threw up. Splat onto the deck and everyone scarpered. We had the whole corner to ourselves. As the Greenman began to just about projectile vomit, people moved further and further away. A crew member suddenly appeared on the top deck, I asked her if she could get me some sick bags, by which time it was probably too late as the floor was covered with the contents of Bill's stomach. Oh, and that last big mug of tea! Yuk! She quickly returned up the stairs with sick bags in one hand, and a bucket of water in the other.

How efficient, I thought, they must be used to this sort of thing.

She proceeded to swill the deck down and swept it quite briskly to remove the offensive display. Suddenly, another crew member appeared at the top of the stairway and yelled,

"What are you doing? There are people down below, right underneath where you've just swilled." Oops!

As the Catamaran turned to head back to shore we were asked to return to our seats. As we took our seats two ladies with very soggy looking hair appeared. I am so sorry but I couldn't contain myself. I took one look at the Greenman, who was still green and white around the gills, and burst out laughing, poor things how awful for them.

One of the men with the women asked if she was all right. "What do you think, how would you feel with bits of someone's breakfast in your hair?" Ouch!

At least that's one Christmas present Bill has bought me that was a total turn around, and I did get a bit of a laugh out of it after all. How sick is that?

www.whalewatch.co.nz

We had come to the conclusion that the best way to see anything interesting in New Zealand was to talk to the locals. Whilst we were in Kaikoura we asked around about any seal colonies, we were told there was one, but it entailed a walk of about 11 kilometres. We thought about the walk, but we had a ferry to catch to the North Island on the 19 December, and to spend another day in Kaikoura may have left us a tad short of time.

On the Wednesday morning, we were back on the road heading north up on State Highway 1 and slightly disappointed that we wouldn't see the seal colony. Oh boy, was Bill intent to get his own back! He was singing even louder than usual.

"On the road again, do di do da da."

Ok, I could stand some of it but the "do di do da das" were driving me around the bend. I put my sun glasses on, foot down and full speed ahead.

It was a winding coastal road with some of the most spectacular scenery on the east coast and awesome views of the Pacific Ocean. Then I was saved from his singing, as we turned one of the bends we saw a sign *Seals next 4 km*. We couldn't believe our eyes, as there they were, seals basking on the rocks. For our convenience, of course, they were right beside a car park. The gift of silence once again filled the van. Ha, bliss!

We parked up and got out of the van rather carefully, so as not to frighten them away. Yet, they just didn't seem bothered by our company at all. It seems they come onto land to recover from their many weeks at sea. It was a spectacular sight, with seals of all sizes and proportions yawning and posing for photographs, whilst basking in the sunshine. We were so glad we hadn't done the 11 kilometre walk. Can you imagine doing the walk and then driving around the corner and seeing this? Back to our map and we discovered we were at Ohau Point, a wonderful rocky, surf lashed strip and home to one of the South Island's largest seal colonies.

We continued on our journey to Blenheim, in preparation for our ferry trip to the North Island and Bill had promised not to sing today. But no such luck! He was humming instead. Annoying!

On the way to Blenheim we discovered a conservation site at Lake Grassmere so we decided to bed down there for the night. It was absolutely pouring down when we arrived so we jumped out of the van ready to hook up, although, we couldn't hook up as conservation sites don't provide electricity. Was this travelling getting to us? I stood there with the electric plug-in in hand and Bill stood looking at me, as though I had, finally, gone completely mad. Unbelievably for Bill, and probably for the first time, words failed him.

The facilities on this conservation site were very good, with toilets and showers. We had a brief respite from the rain and managed a walk along the lake, only to be caught in another downpour. As we were on a conservation site, there was literally nowhere to hang damp clothing, so a soggy night ahead we feared.

There was a salt works at Lake Grassmere and the water turned a pink to purple colour during the summer months. Seawater fresh from the Pacific Ocean was pumped into the lake and the warm north west winds blew across the lake evaporating the water and increasing the concentration of salt, leaving huge white mounds on the shoreline. Apparently, it produces tons of table salt each year.

Porta Potty goes AWOL

It was Thursday, 15 December and Bill's birthday the next day, so as a special surprise I'd booked an apartment, with a Spa bath and all the trimmings, in a motel in Bleinheim. Big mistake, or was it? I shopped on the Friday afternoon for some nice nibbles and wine to have before dinner at the motel. We love our Spanish tapas type food. Our booking was for the Friday and Saturday nights so I suggested we look for a conservation (DoC) site for the Thursday night, near Blenheim. We found a lovely one by the sea at Rarangi, just north of Blenheim. We walked the beach in the afternoon and Bill went scavenging for mussels, which wasn't too difficult in New Zealand, although you are only allowed 50 per person per day. There were large marine notice boards along the coasts and harbours in New Zealand, advising the limits and size of fish you could catch, so it wasn't a free for all!

We settled on our conservation site. I put the porta potty outside of the van whilst I started to prepare our evening meal. As I cooked our meal I could see the potty, out of the corner of my eye, sat on the gravel. Not having this I thought. What a turn off! I jumped out and put the potty over a fence into a field just behind the van. That was better, I could get on with the task in hand. As the evening drew in the site began to fill up with young people; their tents; their guitars; their beer and well who knows what else. We made the decision to make a hasty retreat, as two older, grey gappers, wanting peace and tranquility may not fit in at this particular site. Although, there was a young American couple pulled up beside us and they were lovely and friendly. The others probably were too, but we thought about the possibility of lack of sleep and headed off.

We had noticed a site in Blenheim on the way through so we'd go back there. It was a very big site but not too busy, so would suit our needs for one night. We paid our site fees and hooked up. About an hour after we'd settled in we noticed the porta potty was missing. Oh no, we'd left it behind in the field, where I had happily placed it over the fence out of the way of my 'offence'. As we were looking at about 200 dollars to replace it we hastily jumped into the van. Pushing and shoving everything we'd taken out into any space it would go. We were in such a panic that we only just narrowly averted another disaster. We'd forgotten to unhook the electricity cable. When the van jerked as we set off, we just glared at each other, whose fault was this then? But with no time to waste with accusations, we unhooked and hit the road. Wow! We realized just in time, otherwise we may have taken the electric box with us, that would have been even more expensive than the porta potty.

We arrived back at the site in Rarangi, and luckily the young American couple had noticed we were driving away without our treasured prize, and had tried to flag us down. I do remember waving back to them thinking they were just waving goodbye. As we pulled onto the conservation site we spied the couple. They were sat either side of a small fire, quite happily taking it in turns to stir the pot and singing along to each other. When we alighted from the van they just said,

"Hi, been waiting for ya. Saved ya potty from the warden. He came around and wanted to take it into custody. Saw ya left it behind and tried to flag ya down, but ya just waved at us."

We all had a good laugh and we promised to give them a mention on our blog as a way of thanks. Well there you go guys it's in the book as well. Thank you once again for saving us from going potty over our missing porta potty.

Blenheim – We Shouldn't Be Here!

I was so excited the next morning to surprise Bill, with his birthday treat of a decent bed space and spa bath, in a motel in Blenheim. Unfortunately, he was not at all pleased, as he had planned to go to Nelson for the weekend. Lack of communication? Oops! I had already booked and paid for the accommodation from my own budget. Oh dear! I felt awful. I'd got it wrong, there were bound to be words. We proceeded to find the motel in Blenheim, but Bill was none too happy and I could see him gritting his teeth. As we arrived we pulled over at the motel entrance facing the wrong way, traffic wise, we had no sooner stopped than a little man came running over to us.

"You can't park there like that," he said looking quite angrily at us.

"Are you English?" but before we could reply he said, "thought so."

I said very politely, that we'd missed the entrance to the motel and we were going to reverse back to park up in the motel car park.

"No," he said. "Move now, you need to turn around quickly. If the police come along you'll get a whacking great fine for parking on the wrong side of the road. They're really hot on this one."

We had noticed everyone seemed to park facing the way they were travelling, I had mentioned this to Bill but he had just poo pooed me, and suggested I was being even more paranoid than usual. Lovely! So, we were grateful to have been given this information, even though quite abruptly.

We checked in to a lovely apartment, a real treat, and the Jacuzzi bath was very welcoming indeed. Oh, by the way the angry little man was the owner of the Motel, where we were staying, and was actually, eventually quite pleasant. How people change when there's money involved!

Bill still wasn't happy about our little detour but agreed to have a wander into Blenheim and do some proper Christmas shopping, no animals, mammals or creatures involved. To our surprise, it was the day of the Christmas parade, so off we went to find somewhere for a drink, a bite to eat and comfortable seats, to watch the proceedings. Yet, it didn't feel at all right. Watching what we in Britain would call a summer carnival in brilliant sunshine was ok, but not with Father Christmas and the false snow! It all sort of screws with your mind. We'd been so used to being in Britain at Christmas, with the cold dark winter nights and proper snow (well sometimes).

Christmas seemed a bit false but it was refreshing to notice that Kiwis weren't going overboard the way we do in Britain. Not many Christmas lights around either, but then it was light until quite late in the evening so no point really. In New Zealand Christmas was all about holidays and BBQ's. The false snow was actually melting much faster than the machine could blow it out, most of it didn't even get the chance to hit the ground.

Bill hadn't been happy about being in Blenheim, but thank goodness we were, and one of the few times we'd been glad of our lack of communication. Bill had planned to go to Nelson and onto one of the conservation sites. However, and to our astonishment, the area had the most horrific floods and the site we would have stayed on was flooded so badly some campers and camper vans were stuck for the whole weekend, it had been a very dangerous situation.

It was on Tuesday, 13 December 2011 people were busy preparing for Christmas and the summer holidays and it began to rain. By Wednesday, 14 December a state of emergency was declared as the Matai River rose and began to flood its banks. Sandbags were laid and multiple roads were closed along with State Highway 6. Around Nelson the traffic had become gridlocked. Hundreds of people were evacuated from their homes, as it was feared the slipping hillside might envelop them. As the intense weather moved away from Nelson they began to assess the damage. It was the worst disaster in the region for decades, with Takakas normal annual rainfall of 674 millimetres seen in just two days, and the hills behind Nelson suffered land slips after the deluge. The rain continued until Thursday, 15 December, it was a torrential downpour. The likes of which Takaka hadn't seen in over 500 years and Nelson in 250 years.

When we heard the news, we were quite shocked. Bill looked ashen as he said, "How did you know?"

But I hadn't known. I'd had no idea at all!

Phew, close call, someone must have been watching over us!

We drove from Blenheim on the Sunday morning to Picton, where we were to catch the Interislander Ferry to the North Island on the Monday. We'd already booked our tickets on line, as it was summer time in New Zealand and holiday time, so it was likely to be very busy.

We also booked our site for the Christmas period. Although it had basically been potluck, as we really didn't know where would be best, except we needed to be up north on the North Island.

We later hooked up at the nearest site to the ferry terminal in Picton. It seemed most people were doing the same as us, a quick stop before catching the ferry the next day.

On Monday, 19 December we drove to the ferry port in Picton. We had plenty of time before we sailed. I wonder why? As usual my need to be in good time, in fact ridiculously early. So, we had a tour of this small attractive town on foot and later headed up the side of the beautiful Queen Charlotte sound, to watch the boats and the ferries, whilst we had a bite to eat and plenty of cups of tea.

The weather began to change yet again, it became quite cold, wet and very windy as we made our way back down to the port. My, how busy it was! I think we kept forgetting it was Christmas time and the big holiday in New Zealand, after all it was their summer vacation.

Once on the ferry, little Isaac van was nicely wedged between two very big camper vans, he didn't mind at all, he could certainly hold his own, we were very proud of him. We immediately rushed to the top deck to wave goodbye to the South Island until next year, but that didn't last long as the wind became ferocious and the rain heavier.

I met an elderly guy on the stairs and when he realized we were English he began to apologize for the weather, and told us it was becoming one of the worst summers he could remember.

Well for us, it was a very good summer, after all, we're English!

We had a very uneventful sail to the North Island, no sea creatures, mammals or mermaids for Bill to get excited about! Although I did keep a very close eye on the Greenman for any signs of him going green around the gills!

Chapter 7

Sailing to Christmas on the North Island

We arrived in Wellington later that afternoon. New Zealand's cosmopolitan capital sits majestically at the bottom of the surrounding hills on the one side, and the Cook Strait on the other. We disembarked from the ferry at approximately quarter to six and headed up the west coast to Whanganui, with Isaac rested and ready to rev., and Bill navigating, right way round this time, it was full steam ahead.

"We're on the road again." Oh no! No!

We had booked a campsite at Miranda, a historical fort and small village on the Firth of Thames, for Christmas, and were due there on the 23 December. With Miranda being approximately a drive of 590 kilometres from Wellington, we intended to wind our way up the west coast, doing as much sightseeing and touristy things as time would allow. We eventually found State Highway 1 and made our way north to spend the night at Whanganui, where there's a Quaker settlement we had been told not to miss. We really had to motor on as it was early evening and we were both quite tired. As the evening wore on we somehow lost our way. We couldn't understand it, we had been doing so well, but then at the last toilet stop we had reversed roles. It must have been Bill's singing that put me off driving as I was navigating and Bill was driving. A few knowing looks from Bill and it was all change. A quick call to the settlement to review our directions, and of course, with my excellent driving skills we were there in no time at all, the latter part of the journey had been totally silent! We eventually arrived just before darkness fell and after a warm welcome hooked up the van and enjoyed a good night's rest. The next morning, we were shown around the settlement and thought it was amazing.

Whanganui Quaker Settlement

There are sixteen homes surrounding a residential seminar centre, which is used for retreats and conferences by Quakers and other groups. A Quaker Trust set up in 1975 owns the 20-acre site. There is no settler's ownership of the land, the tenure therefore is not ownership but guardianship. The settlers share all the management responsibilities and work cooperatively using spiritually discerned decision-making. Part of the settlements mission is to find more sustainable ways of living together and developing a permaculture approach to the use of their land.

We loved the settlement, everyone was very friendly and welcoming so we promised we'd be back, but in the meantime, we had to hit the road and head north.

We hadn't planned our next hook up for the night, but we weren't too concerned as it was very easy to find good campsites in New Zealand, with excellent facilities and cleanliness. I loved the peace and quiet and Bill was forever looking for the next bird or any wildlife that enabled him to tick off one of his 'have seen' boxes.

Mount Egmont

We travelled up State Highway 1 and took a left turn onto Highway 3 at Bulls, heading towards New Plymouth we weren't quite sure whether we'd stay there, or push it and travel a little further up the coast. After all, we were eager and excited to be travelling to Christmas. We could see Mount Egmont in the distance just below New Plymouth and had been told not to miss Dawson Falls in the Egmont National Park.

Mount Egmont is a dormant volcano that last erupted in 1755, it rises to 2,518 metres. Even in the summer months the top of the mountain remains white with snow. It was a fantastic sight driving up to it, but the best photographs were actually taken from a few miles away. Three sealed roads climbed the sides of the mountain and all ended a little under half way up at a car park from where the parks 140 kilometres of walking tracks were spread out.

(A "sealed" road is a tarmac surface as distinct from "unsealed" which is stone, gravel and dust.)

As it was getting later into the afternoon, and we still had to find a site to stay for the night, we took one of the lower walks and viewed Dawson Falls. Having had a cup of tea, a quick visit to freshen up at the Dawson Falls visitor centre, and with a perusal of our tourist atlas we found a small campsite at a place called Waiiti. Although we were rather puzzled as to why the site at Waiiti wasn't on the campsite map? We were on the road again, and I was being very quiet as Bill wasn't singing. Sshhh!

Where is Waiiti?

We continued on our journey looking for the sign to the Waiiti camp site, to begin with I'm navigating and Bill's driving. Big mistake. When will we ever learn? We passed the camp site sign heading north. Great won't be long now, as it was early evening and I was beginning to feel a little more than hungry and this does tend to play havoc with my concentration. Then I happened to look back down the road and saw the camp site sign going the other way! We must have missed the turn off. I couldn't believe it, I wouldn't have missed the turn off, would I? Surely there would have been a sign or something wouldn't there?

Bill slammed on the brakes and said, "Drive!"

Mmm! I thought I'd better! There was the sign again which we had just passed and we were heading south.

"We'll be there in no time at all," said Bill, with that I know what I'm doing look. A few miles further along and there was the sign pointing in the other direction again. What on earth was happening? The air in the van was starting to feel quite delicate and I was getting hungrier by the minute!

I then stopped and said, "Ok boss, which way?"

Half an hour later, yes, we were very persistent but evening was creeping in, we took a guess at a left turn and there it was right in front of us. We both looked at each other in astonishment and Bill exclaimed, "Where the heck did that come from, how on earth did we miss it?"

The road we eventually turned down just seemed to appear. Ooh, something weird here maybe we shouldn't stay! Hunger and tiredness by then had taken over and won the battle, otherwise we may have scampered away very quickly.

A woman came out of the office at the campsite and wanted to know what we were doing, as we were peering rather hesitantly over the closed gate and into the site. We told her we'd been looking for the site for ages.

She half laughed and said, "Hook up wherever you want, the kitchens over there," took our money and off she went. She seemed very nice though!

We found it to be a pretty site, although the facilities weren't the best, but they were more than adequate. We were then amazed to see shipping containers turned into small habitable units for holidaymakers and tourists, absolutely incredible, so innovative. Having seen the use of the shipping containers in Christchurch this was another brilliant idea.

After a hastily cooked and quickly eaten meal and with very little light left we decided to have a walk down to the beach, which was just in front of the campsite. We had read that there was a colony of blue penguins in the area and thought it would be fantastic to see these little fellows again. The evening was closing in fast, the sun was setting, and it soon became the twilight hour. We hadn't really noticed the darkness closing in on us, as we'd been so busy scouring around the beach to try and catch a glimpse of a blue penguin in its natural habitat. The excitement must have given me a false sense of security as I suddenly realized it was by then quite dark. This threw me a bit. No, a lot actually! My sense of direction in the daylight was awful so imagine me in the dark! However, we had been sensible enough to take torches with us. Ok, well I say 'we' it was the boy scout! About turn! We scurried across the pebbles and rocks, tumbling and falling with muttering and moaning. Bill marched on in front and at times I could only just see a flicker from the beam of his torch.

There were feeble cries from me, "Bill, Bill, it's the wrong way, wait, you're taking us to the sea. Wait, it's the wrong way."

The only retort I received from Bill was, "Come on, keep up. I know where I'm going."

Oh really? I thought.

Yes, he did as it happened. As we approached the campsite I pulled myself together, straightened my hair and said a very confident "good evening" as we walked past the lady who had checked us in. I then realised, as I followed her gaze to my feet and sandals, that they were completely obliterated with a black, sandy, muddy gunge from the beach. I pretended it wasn't there, ran my hands through my hair again, smiled and flopped my way back to the van, leaving a small trail of mud and sand in my wake. Whatever must she have thought we'd been up to on the beach in the dark?

After a hot shower we retired for the night. I could hear the sound of a gentle breeze swirling around the van and in the distance the waves crashing onto the beach. Otherwise it was very quiet and very dark, so I snuggled down and pulled the duvet over my head and thought of how quickly we could make a hasty retreat in the morning.

The Waitomo Valley

How strange! We had everything packed up, drained down and breakfast eaten by 9 o'clock the next morning, actually quite early for us. We found our way back onto State Highway 3 and were rather hastily heading towards the Waitomo valley and the Waitomo Top 10 Holiday Park. We arrived at the site much earlier than we had expected to. I think we both got a bit spooked the night before, serves us right for swanning around on the beach in the dark. The Waitomo site was quite large with very good facilities, but as it was Thursday, 22 December, nearly Christmas, and, of course being the summer holidays, it was very busy. The barbeques were on the go all evening and children were running around chatting and laughing with excitement. Kiwis get the full whammy with the summer holidays and Christmas all rolled into one, but some told us it makes winter rather a drag as they've nothing to look forward to.

The next morning, we walked up to the Waitomo Caves Discovery Centre, where we settled for the bush walk, and viewed some of the smaller caves with streams running through. It was a lovely early morning walk and we enjoyed it very much. Just what we needed after the excitement of the last 24 hours! There were larger caves there for guided tours, but I'm afraid both finance and time swayed our decision not to visit them.

www.waitomo.com

Miranda for Christmas

We were on the road again continuing on State Highway 3 towards Hamilton, from there we travelled across country on State Highway 26 to Morrinsville. We then turned off onto State Highway 27, up alongside the Hapuakohe Range until we reached the smaller roads, which would lead us to our destination for Christmas, 'Miranda' on the Thames Firth. I suffered in silence though, as Bill serenaded me with, '♪On the road again, do di do da da♪'. I needed a plan to get him to change his tune.

I put my sunglasses on and pushed my foot down on the accelerator as we approached a wide bend. Round we go, nearly on two wheels. I drove even harder out of the bend. Brakes were screeching as I hit them with full force on the next bend. Bill started to scream as I overtook a Mercedes Benz. I think it must have been the big truck coming the other way that scared him. But Isaac did pull his wing mirrors in as we scraped along the side of the truck. At least he'd stopped singing. Ah ha! Got him. Isaac had responded wonderfully taking on the challenge, even he was fed up with the singing.

My daydream was over as I heard a voice in the distance say,

"Would you like a mint?" I turned and looked at Bill, who was smiling and obviously in his own little world.

"No thank you," I replied. I looked up the road and across to the mountain range, what fantastic scenery and wonderful day dreams!

We were delighted we'd chosen Miranda, as it had something for both of us. It was by the sea which was an enticement, but the thermal pools won me over, and the bird watching would be great for Bill.

The Firth of Thames is an arm of the Hauraki Gulf separating South Auckland from the Coromandel Peninsula. It was very windswept and comprised of land built up by successive deposits of

shell banks. Much had been converted to farmland, but newer shell banks could be seen in the making along what's known as the Sea Bird Coast. Situated on the coastal road was the Miranda Shore Bird centre. Almost a quarter of all known species of migrating shore birds visit the region, and 30,000 strong flocks of wrybill and plover over winter at this internationally significant site. During the southern summer, September to March, arctic migrants can be seen – notably bar tailed godwits and lesser knots – who fly 15,000 kilometres from Alaska and Siberia.
www.miranda-shorebird.org.nz

After a good journey, despite the singing, we arrived at Miranda quite late in the afternoon. The site was lovely, very clean and quite big – we found a lovely corner plot which gave us a bit more space with a nice grass area. We were becoming wiser as we visited different sites. Look for a corner plot, always bigger and sometimes a nice patch of grass. Look for a picnic bench and if there is one move it next to your van to make a delightful eating area. Although, we soon learned that you must hang something on the bench or it would go walk about very quickly. I think it's called ownership! A bench was quite important to us, as it was a wonderful opportunity to relish our meals outdoors in the evenings, dinner 'alfresco' – but of course!

We were becoming quite possessive as it was quite annoying when we went out touring or visiting for the day, and arrived back to find, what we'd claimed as our bench, had gone AWOL. Then later, when we were hot and tired after our day out, the people we'd conversed with on the site would often take great pleasure in telling us who had taken 'YOUR' bench. The fun would then begin, as Bill would prowl around the site looking for 'OUR' bench.

We soon found Miranda's thermal pool and couldn't resist an early evening dip. It was warm and soothing and just what the doctor ordered. Oh, how much truth there was to be in those words of wisdom!

We later drove along the coast to Kaiaua to familiarize ourselves with the area and drive past the Sea Bird Centre. There was a part of the shoreline where self-contained camper vans could park, for up to two nights. It was very popular, as it was busy the whole time we were staying at Miranda. It was at Kaiaua we first saw the Kiwi Christmas Tree, (pohutukawa) at least we hadn't noticed any before this. The pohutukawa is a coastal evergreen tree of the myrtle family, with its beautiful crimson flowers, this tree often appeared on greetings cards and featured in songs.

We bought an ice cream from a little hut style shop across the road from the beach. We thought the young boy had made a mistake as he piled the ice cream into the cones, until it was impossible to get anymore in them or onto them. They were massive, we'd never seen such large ice creams and so cheap. I had the Hokey Pokey ice cream and loved it. It was a vanilla ice cream with small solid lumps of honeycomb toffee, gorgeous. But there was so much of it, I could hardly waddle onto the beach afterwards. Ah, but at last Bill was multi-tasking, there he was sat under a Kiwi Christmas tree, bird watching and eating an ice-cream, all at the same time!

It was Saturday, 24 December and the site was beginning to fill up. We'd enjoyed a leisurely alfresco breakfast and a dip in the thermal pool. We were preparing for lunch when a couple arrived with a very large caravan and parked next but one to our plot. Soon after they arrived they came along to our van and introduced themselves. They informed us that they had reserved the site between ourselves and them, as their friends would be arriving later in the afternoon, and they had a very big van, by the way they said, "It's a VERY big van"!

Ok we got the message. We waited in anticipation and had a bit of a giggle as we watched for this "very big van" to arrive. Maybe they were just being sarcastic, because we were sooo small, we tittered again.

Oh yes, it was huge! We heard it arrive. In fact, the whole campsite probably heard it. It was being towed by a whacking great Range Rover type truck. They parked up as we stood with eyes popping and mouths open. They began to settle in and just to make sure we knew how huge their van was, no bus, no artic, they started to push buttons and the sides came out! The whole great monster just got bigger and bigger. I don't think our little van would have filled the driver's cab of their tow truck! We had a good laugh though, know your place and all that! Next thing they were out on the grass and the G and T's were flowing, hope they don't start singing I thought! Especially not 'We're on the road again, do di do da da," I would probably have screamed!

We were saddened later in the day when we heard there had been another big earthquake in Christchurch, the day before, on 23 December. It had been at a magnitude of 6.2, which meant that buildings already weakened by previous quakes and shocks would probably go into the red zone. There had also been more significant rock falls. The airport at Christchurch had been evacuated and people were asked to stay off the roads as crevices and holes reappeared. We contacted our friends in Christchurch to check that everyone was ok, and were informed that they were. We were relieved, but our hearts went out to them, as yet more fear and destruction would ensue. I must admit we were relieved we hadn't been in Christchurch at the time, and did count our blessings at yet another near miss! The people of Christchurch would stay in our thoughts and our hearts until we returned.

It was Christmas Day and what better way to start the day than with a dip in the thermal pool, followed by a lovely alfresco breakfast. But to really top it all, Bill cooked our Christmas Day lunch and I didn't lift a finger. Roast chicken with all the trimmings, scrumptious. We did laugh when he told me of the tussle he'd had in the kitchen, fighting to keep his oven space, and watching his bird didn't disappear, as a lot of people had the same idea. What happened to the barbequing that we were told was the tradition on Christmas Day? Maybe someone was testing our English sense of humour. We'd even bought decorations for the van. No sorry, I bought decorations for the van. I still don't know if Bill was too happy at poor little Isaac being covered in tinsel and glitter, not usually my style, but you have to show the big boys, don't you? We were the only slightly over decorated van on the site. Well, I had been feeling slightly home sick thinking about the excitement of my lovely grandchildren back home, in Britain and Spain.

Whilst we'd both been Christmas shopping, separately of course as we both like surprises. Well some surprises are ok, and due to our lack, once again, of communication we each bought a box of

Christmas Crackers, so we had 24 crackers for two people. How crackers was that? We thought of passing them around the site but had a feeling they may come in useful later on. How, in England, could you comprehend going camping or caravanning for Christmas and to top it all, eat Christmas Day lunch alfresco.

We met a lovely Kiwi couple, who were staying in their caravan just across from our plot, they had introduced themselves quite soon after arriving. It was really good to chat with local people and we had some interesting conversations with them about New Zealand and why we were there. They had their caravan parked on the site all the year round and used it quite often. They pointed to our 'big neighbours' and 'tutted' at the size of their van. They then very quickly informed us, that they themselves, would only ever buy a caravan from the UK, as the quality was so much better than from any other country. Amazing, well done the UK caravan industry! They seemed to look out for us with a wave and hello and were we ok? They were also pretty good at watching where our bench disappeared to when we were off the site. Whenever we returned from a journey, they would rush over and give us an in-depth report as to the possible whereabouts of OUR bench, very surreptitiously of course.

A few days previously I'd noticed a bite on my foot just below my ankle, and I had given it the same respect I would any mosquito bite, as I had thought that's what it was. While bathing in the thermal pool on Christmas Day, I had noticed a red line running from the bite and up my leg, and a rather large lump had appeared on the inside of my thigh. I knew this was possibly an infection, but I felt fine and the bite wasn't big or swollen, just turning a little black. I thought it could wait and then tried to convince myself that maybe I'd sat in the thermal pool too long. Ah well, you know what thought did. Who was I kidding? I hadn't mentioned anything to Bill but on Boxing Day I shared my concerns, yet at the same time, tried to reassure him that I'd be fine until after the Bank Holiday. Deep down I knew this wasn't right but didn't want to cause any alarm. Bill became quite anxious and on reflection quite rightly so.

Off he marched to the site office to get some advice about medical treatment in the area, and was told the only help would be at the Thames Hospital some 35 kilometres away. I protested quite strongly, as it was Boxing Day, and I didn't want anyone to be troubled by me and it could probably wait. But yes, that little voice had been nagging me again saying "stop being stubborn." To no avail, I knew quite rightly, it was the sensible thing to do. Bill seemed to suddenly have an urgency about this. I think I was just in denial. I hate having anything wrong with me. Sometimes the spirit tries to lead and instinct kicks in, but do we listen? If we would just sometimes listen to that small still voice!

We arrived at the hospital in Thames and soon located the Emergency Department, although I knew it wasn't fine I still felt a pang of guilt being there on Boxing Day. As we approached the department there was a notice, *Waiting time 4 hours.*

"Maybe we could come back tomorrow," I said.

Bill's answer was a plain, "No."

As we entered I looked around and the people I saw waiting seemed to have real problems. I felt quite a fraud and so approached the reception desk rather sheepishly. I kept thinking to myself actually this isn't urgent, it's a mossie bite, but that little voice in the back of my head kept saying even louder now, "Oh yes, it is urgent."

I gave my details and was asked to take a seat. With a 4 hour wait I suggested that Bill should go and get himself a cup of tea, I didn't have to say it twice.

Off he went with a, "Won't be long, see you soon."

He'd no sooner turned the corner when a nurse called me into a side room to assess the problem. She was very nice and didn't even look at the bite. I thought, oh dear it's not serious enough after all. I did feel silly, but the little voice was still there saying "Ah you wait and see." So much so that it began to disturb me. Seated once again in the waiting area and with no sign of Bill, my heart began to beat a little faster and my hands became hot and clammy. I looked around at the other people in the room. I often do this. What are their lives like? Where do they live? Are they happy? Then I realised I was in displacement mode, to take my mind off myself. A few minutes later my name was called to see the doctor. Oh dear, all those people had been there before me. I felt embarrassed. I didn't dare look at any of them.

I did my usual sorry to bother you on a Bank Holiday, blahdy, blah, and explained to the doctor what the problem was, still feeling a bit of a fraud.

To which he answered, "That's what we're here for. Right let's see this bite then."

I had a plaster over the bite, it wasn't big like some bites you get abroad or even at home, it was slightly raised with the centre turning black.

On removing the plaster, the doctor's face changed, and he said, "Wow, we do have a problem here!"

I was dumbfounded, as the bite wasn't swollen or red just a biggish black spot. I was astonished. As it transpired to be a spider bite probably that of a poisonous spider. The doctor suggested the Poisonous Australian White Spotted Tail Spider. Oh! Great I thought, but how and when? Within minutes I was on an antibiotic intravenous drip, given two large oral antibiotics and a prescription for a two-week course of the same.

The doctor then looked at me and said, "I'm so glad you came today otherwise you may have been in big trouble."

Bill arrived back to the waiting area of the Emergency Department, and of course I wasn't there.

When he enquired, they said, "Oh just go through there, she's on a drip." He said he felt an awful panic and nausea fill his stomach. Oh! No not again! When he appeared, he looked ashen, and I had to reassure him it was an antibiotic drip, and that I was fine. I then ushered Bill back to the waiting area before he got any paler and collapsed on the floor, or some such thing! When the drip had finished, I was discharged, but told to go straight back if I felt at all unwell. When I walked back into the waiting area Bill looked relieved. I thanked him profusely for making sure I had the bite checked out. We left the Thames Hospital feeling very humble and subdued, but grateful for their speedy medical attention.

On arriving back at the site the Kiwi couple, with the caravan opposite ours, were curious to find out where we'd been, they seemed quite concerned. How had they known something was wrong? We'll never know, except maybe our hasty retreat earlier that morning. When we told them about the bite they began to relate some horror stories to us about people they had heard of being bitten by the same type of spider.

One chap was ill for over a year and lost his arm. Another woman got the flesh-eating disease (necrotic arachnidism), and did we know they love living in buildings under bedding or clothes. Oh and by the way your bench went that way, pointing across the park. When I turned around, to see where Bill had disappeared to, he had half the van stripped out, remember it was only a small van, and our bedding was hanging on trees being whacked.

We all just stood watching him, aghast at this behavior, but as Bill said later, "Had the culprit been living with us, travelling around in our little van and one evening just felt a little hungry?" Ouch!

The Australian White Spotted Tailed Spider has a long cigar shaped, dark grey abdomen, with a creamy white spot on the tip of its tail. They vary in size from 12mm to 20mm long. They can be found in cool dark areas such as under bark, leaves or litter etc. They can commonly be seen in houses and other buildings, as they mainly eat other spiders and are mostly active at night. They're slow moving and will roam great distances for prey. There is currently much conjecture regarding the effects of the bite from this spider. It has been linked with a spreading skin ulceration known as necrotic arachnidism, which as yet has no cure. It is likely that any disease caused from the spider's bite, isn't from the venom, but from the bacteria present in the spider's fangs, at the time of the bite.

I had a rest day the next day, whilst Bill meandered along the coast to do some more bird watching, and later he had a final dip in the thermal pool. I'd missed out on that one.

We packed up the following day and said a fond farewell to Miranda, and the people we'd met, and hopefully leave our friend the white spotted tailed travelling companion behind. We hadn't found Mr Nippy Tail, and came to the conclusion that our late evening scramble up the beach over stones and leaves, at Waiiti, a couple of days earlier, may have disturbed a female with her eggs. Who knows?

Chapter 8

Summer Gathering in the Chosen Valley

On Wednesday, 28 December we travelled across country and slightly north to the Quaker Summer Gathering at the Chosen Valley near Drury, a Christian-camp in the Ararimu valley, with a range of accommodation options.

The Chosen Valley is an inter-denominational Christian organization, administered by a Board of Trustees and run by paid staff. There were lots of outdoor activities to suit all ages such as; adventure playground; bush walks; Burma trail; balance island; flying fox; kayaks; orienteering; rafting; rope maze; table tennis; slingshots; team balance; trampoline; waterslide; trolleys volleyball; archery and more.

"It is a real joy to serve God here surrounded by His creation and especially when the air is filled with the sound of young people (and adults too) having fun and relishing the atmosphere of the temporary communities that camping is all about"

www.chosenvalleycamp.org.nz

We'd booked the week to get to know New Zealand Quakers, as it was a brilliant opportunity to meet Friends from all over the country. We'd also offered to present the Quaker story and the Testimonies talk to the group. We had reserved a double room. It would be a nice break from putting the bed up and down in the van. Also, no need for the porta potty in the middle of the night and less chance of losing it again! Unfortunately, we'd been allocated a room which was the sitting room of one of the cottages, with a sofa bed, and the main door of the unit stepped directly into the room, so there would be through traffic! We made the decision to sleep in the van, as we preferred a little more privacy.

Well, it wasn't too bad in our little van, but it was always the same, the lure of a proper bed was very enticing.

We made ourselves known to the organizing committee and received a programme and our rota duties. We were being fully catered for, so everyone had duties for the week, laying of tables, tidying up, setting up rooms etc.. Bill was given the duty of helping to set up the dining room for evening meals, and I was to help set up the Meeting for Worship room, and tidy the craft room. Although, on the first evening watching the Chef struggle to serve the food as the queue grew longer and longer, I decided to help him, which he seemed very grateful for. The food was very good and the kitchen staff were lovely.

It was during our first day at the Chosen Valley that the rains began. It rained, and rained, and rained, and for 6 days everyone was wet, wet, wet. Isaac was getting muddier and muddier and even more threatening he seemed to be sinking deeper and deeper into the grass where we were parked. There had been no other option than the grass parking as this was where the hook up was and no hook up, no electricity, which would have meant us blundering around in the dark every night and you know what happens when we do that!

Although, the rain and soggy wet clothes didn't deter our Kiwi friends, especially the younger ones, they were very gung-ho and it was business as usual; kayaking, archery, rafting and sliding down the muddy embankment and splash into the lake with lots of whoops and squeals. There was Salsa dancing lessons, bush tramps, crafts and knitting, fellowship, Meeting for Worship, concerts, talks, discussions, epilogues each evening before bedtime drinks, and New Year's Eve dancing.

An Epilogue: Each evening before retiring we would join together and one or two would bring their thoughts, their prayers, a favourite reading or poetry or maybe play a piece of music. Just 30 minutes with words and music, in the silence of the coming together, was a relaxing and wonderful end to the day.

During the first few days at the gathering we felt slightly wary and uncomfortable, as it was difficult to blend with some of this group. There were those who were lovely and welcoming, yet others seemed a little distant and distrusting. I don't think they realized our intentions were good and we weren't freewheeling. In fact, they kept asking us to pay for our week at the Chosen Valley and didn't seem to believe us when we explained that we'd paid six weeks previously! However, the money was soon found by the lovely Resident Friends, Ginna and Davie, who were volunteering at the meeting house in Auckland. It had been allocated to the wrong column in the accounts!

We had previously contacted the organizing committee of the gathering to offer a session on the Quaker story presentation and the Testimonies talk. However, to our great disappointment we'd been left off the programme. Bill was quite upset and approached the committee. It was eventually resolved and we were offered a couple of places on the programme for later in the week. We certainly appreciated this as it opened up discussions with people, some of whom had misunderstood part of the Quaker history. It also allowed us to reach out to other meetings on the North Island to book dates to visit them later on in our travels. All in all, we had an interesting and enlightening time at the Summer Gathering and felt more at home and accepted by the end of the week.

The Quaker Centre, Auckland

With the fun and companionship of the Summer Gathering over we were off to Auckland next, and hopefully to meet up again with some of the people from the Chosen Valley event.

Ginna and Davie had kindly offered us a bed for four nights in return for cover to allow them a day off. Deal done, we jumped at the opportunity after having survived a very wet and soggy week in the campervan. We arrived at the Quaker Centre in Auckland at about lunchtime on Wednesday, 4 January, 2011, with a very warm welcome from our delightful hosts.

Auckland is New Zealand's largest city and was built on approximately 50 small volcanoes sprawled across a very narrow isthmus. Its nick named the 'city of sails,' as most weekends the two harbours, Waitemata and Manukau, are a spectacle of brightly coloured sails as the sailing boats wind their way around the bays.

Although it's a large city it had kept a very relaxed and laid back atmosphere. There were classic boutiques, restaurants, cafes and all the usual shopping you would expect but without the hassle. It's one of the least densely populated cities in the world, with twice the space of London, yet home to just over a million people. Auckland is also the world's largest Polynesian city, as around 11% of the population claim to be of Maori descent.

The Quaker centre was situated on Mount Eden Road, next to the Meeting house in a suburb of Auckland, with accommodation for visitors on a bed and breakfast basis, two twin rooms plus an annexe double room. There were also two meeting rooms, which community groups used. Friends Centre was occupied and looked after by Voluntary Resident Friends, the position we were to have held in Christchurch if the earthquakes hadn't severely damaged the buildings.

By this time, Bill had severe gardening withdrawal symptoms, so we soon found some gardening equipment, and with the permission of our hosts, we concentrated on the garden for the rest of the day, and at last, the sun was now shining. We cleared, weeded, pruned, cut the grass and did a general overall tidy up, being very careful as some of the plants were unknown to us. Our hosts were quite relieved, as gardening wasn't really their bag, although they were a dab hand at repairs and the general running of the centre.

The following morning, we were given a tour of the centre and the meeting house and brought up to speed with the day-to-day running. Later, we decided to visit the nearest shopping suburb of Auckland. Ginna and Davie talked us through a walk via some of the back roads into the city, also where to go and what to see within a very small radius of Mount Eden Road. Bill was once again having problems with his iPad, he was becoming quite frustrated, as it just wouldn't behave itself and do what he wanted. Off we went, to take a look around this area of the city, and whilst there see if we could find a Telecom shop, and hoped they could help Bill with his iPad. We took the instructions we'd been given and as the rain arrived once again, we kitted ourselves out with the usual kagoul, boots etc.

On our way to the main shopping area we passed a Hell's Angels house on the left, we walked on the right! It was a big building with big gates and a fence and a very obvious Hells Angels sign. Interesting!

We walked up and down the shopping area looking for the Telecom shop, but to no avail. We made several enquiries in different shops as to the whereabouts of the it, but came up with blank looks. So, we wandered up and down the streets and ventured into one or two charity shops.

As soon as I started to look at anything Bill crept up behind me and said, in no uncertain terms, "No, no room."

We were just about to give up on the Telecom shop when it suddenly appeared, we had probably walked past it several times. We were pleased to have at last found the shop, and as we entered there were two very nice young men stood behind the counter, smiling at us with a real welcoming look. They winked at each other. We smiled and I thought, oh how friendly, then before we could say anything one of the young men said,

"English?" Wow how did they know? Did we look so lost, or just English?

Bill said, "Actually yes, that's amazing how did you know? We don't look that English, do we?"

They both smiled again and at the same time said, "Nice jackets!"

Uh? What did that mean? After all we had our kagouls, scarves, and boots on, and an umbrella each too. Now this is the clue, when we left the shop we looked around the street. It was pouring down with rain and the Kiwis had umbrellas, but were only wearing shorts and t-shirts. Yep, it's January and summer in New Zealand, quite humid and warm. After all, it is a tropical island! They saw us coming covered head to toe in waterproofs. Well, at least we made their day and gave them a good laugh.

We stood in for the Resident Friends and looked after the centre for a couple of nights, to allow them to travel to an event in Dunedin on the South Island. During this time, I bit the bullet and rang my Aunty Betty, who lived just outside Auckland. I hadn't seen, or spoken to her for over 50 years. It seemed incredible that my relatives, Aunty, Uncle and two cousins had returned to the UK on several occasions, but I had never met up with them. Something amiss somewhere I reckon.

When I rang Aunty Betty she was delighted to hear from us, and we arranged a trip over to see her the next day. I had a very cheerful and tearful reunion with her, and to my great surprise and happiness, my cousin Christine arrived. It was a truly blessed time. We chatted and swapped stories of our lives. Bill sat there drinking tea and eating sandwiches. I couldn't decide whether he looked amused or bemused, but he seemed really interested to hear us exchanging our news. We bid them a fond farewell with promises to see them again. It had been unsettling and quite bizarre, but well worth it to be reunited with my Kiwi family.

Chapter 9

A Journey to Where the Spirits Leap

Matakohe and the Kauri Museum

With the Resident Friends back in situ, we attended Meeting for Worship on the Sunday, and planned to hit the road again this time heading further north to Matahoke.

I couldn't believe it, he's singing again and I'm trying to study the map to get us out of Auckland. "♪ On the road again, do de, do da do ♪."

"Bill please, you're going to drive me potty with that song, you're not even in tune," I exclaimed!

"What, don't you like it? Are you going to go AWOL same as the porta potty?"

He replied, with a touch of sarcasm in his voice.

I folded my arms, gave him one of my looks and put my sunglasses on. Don't ask me how the glasses were going to help!

We intended to travel on State Highway 16 via Helensville, although we had terrible navigational problems leaving Auckland. You've got it in one. I was navigating and couldn't believe how 'WE' managed to steer ourselves out of the city only to end up back in the centre again. I insisted the map must be out of date, and after all I couldn't read the map properly because of his singing. After a few choice words, I once again became the driver, and with Bill's brilliant navigational skills we were soon passing through Helensville on State Highway 16. We joined State Highway 1 at Wellsford and had a tea stop at Kaiwaka, where there were great picnic facilities. It was a lovely quiet Sunday afternoon so it was nice to sit by the river and sip our mugs of tea. We were soon on the road again, and onwards, onto State Highway 12 to Matakohe and the Kauri Tree Museum.

On arrival, we found the lovely Matakohe Holiday Park with its incredible views and only about 350 metres from the Kauri Museum. It was very quiet and nowhere near the number of tourists we'd expected. We hooked up, did our once a week 'let's empty the fridge', and settled in for the night. The following morning, we visited the Kauri Museum. Along the same road as the museum were little wooden buildings, as we passed them we peeped inside and saw an old-fashioned Post Office and Telephone Exchange, it took us back to another era.

Well, what can we say about the Kauri Museum? The kauri tree was truly majestic and can have a circumference of over 13 metres. The kauri tree industry was massive for the pioneer Kiwi settlers in New Zealand, cutting it down, transporting it with bullock carts, milling it and then shipping it. It was part of the European land settler's clearance as well as a vibrant industry in the 19th century and the early part of the 20th century. The kauri tree can live up to 3,000 years and some trees, long dead, had been dug up from swamps, dried out and milled so there's some very old timber in many New Zealand buildings and wooden artifacts. Gum that oozed from the tree wounds was also an associated industry, it was used to make varnish and linoleum in the early days, but later was prized and polished as jewellery and ornaments.

The kauri tree – kauri is the Maori name – or the Agathis australis, is New Zealand's largest and most famous native tree. It's a huge conifer and grows in the sub-tropical northern part of the North Island. The kauri – podocarp – cone bearing hardwood forests are among the most ancient in the world.

The largest kauri tree in existence is Tane Mahuta, Maori for "Lord of the Forest", with a circumference of 4.4 metres and almost 17.7 metres to the first branch. The oldest kauri tree is estimated to be 2,000 years old. This is Te Matua Ngahere, "Father of the Forest" and has a diameter of over 5mtrs, the widest of any surviving kauri tree. A fully-grown kauri can reach 60 metres and have a diameter of more than 5 metres.

The displays in the museum focused on makeshift settlements around logging camps, the gum fields and the lives of merchants, who were among the few to be able to afford to buy kauri furniture. All of the furniture on display was truly magnificent. You think you've seen the best piece and then you see something even more beautiful, and more majestic. The Kauri Museum is a definite must do, such incredible furniture, such a large tree.

www.kauri-museum.com

Later in the afternoon we travelled onwards to look for a real kauri tree in the Waipoia Kauri Forest. The forest was declared a sanctuary in 1952 and had been maintained by the Waipoua Forest Trust, a community based volunteer organization. There is serious help needed in their effort of conservation. The forest had two of the largest living trees, the 'Lord of the Forest' and the 'Father of the Forest'.

It began to rain, visibility wasn't great, and as we neared Waipoua Kauri Forest, on the next leg of our journey up to Rawene, the weather worsened and it became a downpour, as the driving rain fought with Isaac's windscreen wipers. Once we reached the forest, we decided not to let the weather deter us from actually seeing the kauri tree, in its natural environment. So, of course being British, raincoats on, boots on and brollies to hand we headed off into the forest. Everyone in there seemed to be making a hasty retreat towards their parked cars and vans. But not us, no, we had sailed the high seas to see this and we weren't going to be put off by a little bit of rain, really though, it was a whole load of a downpour. What an incredible experience, it was well worth it, even though we had to watch we didn't slip or slide on the wet boardwalk, as we made our way along to the kauri tree. Then suddenly, wow, there it was in all its true magnificence as it dwarfed everything else in the forest; the kauri tree, 'the Father of the Forest'. Wow! The Kauri Forest was wondrous and majestic even in the driving rain.

Rawene

After a really good soaking in the Kauri Forest, we carried on up State Highway 12 to Rawene, which is half way up Hokianga

Harbour at the tip of Herd's Point. We hooked up at the Rawene Holiday Park, which was on a hilltop and sheltered by native bush, but with magnificent views over the harbour. It was an easy walk into the town and whilst looking around in the evening we decided to eat out, it wasn't too expensive and our excuse was we were both tired. We were clocking up quite a few kilometres each day, but more than that, it was at times quite taxing, not quite sure where we were going, who's driving/navigating, and what we would find when we eventually got there! The one really good thing, and something we began to expect and appreciate was the friendly, polite, and enthusiastic nature of the local people we met at each of our stops.

Rawene is an old settler's town, much reduced, but had been a centre for the logging trade in its day. After a pleasant meal and a much-needed good sleep we opted for a reasonable walk the next morning. We went down and through the town, intending to stock up with groceries on the way back, but then we discovered the boardwalk trail through the Mangrove forest. I found it extremely interesting how the trees survived in all that salt water. We then made the decision to stay another night at this lovely little town. Some of the sites we stayed on were very busy, mainly the big ones with pools, but the out of the way ones in the smaller towns were relatively quiet. We came to the conclusion that most tourists just passed through the smaller towns, but it was our preference to stay and enjoy the tranquility

Mangroves are a diverse group of woody trees and shrubs that inhabit the shallow intertidal, (the area between tide mark above water at low tide and underwater at high tide), margins of sheltered coastal and estuarine environments. Growing in the zone between mean sea level and high tide, they have a variety of special adaptations that allow them to flourish in an environment which is too harsh for most other plant species. Mangroves are associated with warm tropical and sub-tropical climates, but there are a few species that survive in cold climates.

The presence of mangrove trees creates a different physical and biological condition to those of the surrounding mud flats, or those provided by other estuarine plants eg. saltmarsh or seagrass. The unique mangrove habitat provides a range of environmental services and functions. The mangrove plant and its root system slow the flow of water, allowing sediment to settle, and binding the surrounding mud. Mangroves also break up waves and prevent them reaching the shore. As a result, they play an important role in erosion control and shoreline protection.

Cape Reigna - Where the Tasman Sea Battles with the Pacific Ocean

The next morning, we travelled further north to Kaitaia, to meet up with some isolated Quakers whom we'd met at the Summer Gathering. We enjoyed a lovely bring and share meal and Meeting for Worship afterwards. Our hosts gave us a tour of their amazing garden and grounds with olive trees, vines, apples, citrus and soft fruits, as well as a big vegetable patch. It's very Pacific this far north and definitely a Kiwi lifestyle being close to, and hands on, with the earth. We had a really lovely evening and enjoyed chatting, and exchanging news and stories, with these welcoming and interesting people. We said our fond farewells and made our way to a local site for the night before leaving in the morning for Cape Reigna (Ninety Mile Beach).

We arose to sunshine the following morning, and with the Pacific Ocean on the one side and the Tasman Sea on the other we joined State Highway 1F, to travel up to the furthest point north on the North Island. We drove along a narrow 100-kilometre-long finger road with consolidated and grassed over dunes. It's known as "the tail of the fish".

"The Tail of the Fish" – "Te Hika o te Ika"

Maui was a demi god who lived in Hawaiiki, he possessed magic powers that not all of his family knew about. One day when he was very young he hid in the bottom of his brothers' boat, in order to go fishing with them. Once out at sea Maui was discovered by his brothers, but they were not able to take him back to shore as Maui had made use of his magic powers, making the shore line appear to be much further away than it actually was. The brothers continued rowing, and once they were far out into the ocean Maui dropped his magic fish hook over the side of the Waka. After a while he felt a strong pull on the line, it was very strong, so he called on his brothers to help him. After much pulling and straining suddenly up to the surface came Te Ika a Maui – the fish of Maui – known today as the North Island of New Zealand. The South Island is known as Te Waka a Maui – the Waka (canoe) of Maui and Stewart Island (which lies at the bottom of New Zealand) Te Punga a Maui – Maui's Anchor, it was the anchor holding Maui's Waka whilst he pulled the giant fish.

Te Rerenga Wairua – Place of the Leaping Spirits

The most northerly point of the North Island is Cape Reigna, where it is said that the spirits of the Maori dead depart. They begin their journey along Ninety Mile Beach, (which actually isn't 90 miles it's approximately 65 miles long), slide down the cliff edge and then leap from the roots of an 800-year-old pohutukawa tree, the Kiwi Christmas tree, and into the ocean. They climb out again onto 'Ohaua' the highest of the Three King Islands to bid farewell before returning to their ancestors in Hawaiiki.

The Three King Islands are about 57 kilometres north of the rocky shore of New Zealand's North Island. They were named by the Dutch explorer Abel Tasman who had become the first European known to have seen New Zealand. Tasman anchored at the islands whilst searching for water. As it was the Twelfth Night Feast of the Epiphany, the day the biblical Three Kings known as the wise men, visited Christ the child, he named the islands accordingly. Tasman found the islands to be inhabited by Maori, but since approximately 1840 they have been uninhabited.

We arrived at Cape Reigna in the wind and rain. We had left that beautiful sunny morning behind us, as we travelled up and up to the top of the North Island. We had been so looking forward to reaching this point. A lot of people reach this part of the Island by travelling up the 90-mile beach, either with organized day trips on specially designed buses, or under their own steam in four by four vehicles or the like. It's not unknown for some to attempt it in the wrong vehicle and get completely stuck. Our contract for the campervan stated quite clearly 'you must not drive up the 90-mile beach in the van.' It could have been very exciting to do so, but we would either have got lost or sunk into the quick sands of the Te Paki stream.

At last we had reached our destination, parked the van and did a quick toilet stop. We were very excited, so off we went with binoculars, camera and jackets in hand, as we headed down the 800-metre-long trail to Cape Reigna lighthouse. It was eerily quiet as we passed very few people on the trail and no wonder because we couldn't see a thing, with driving rain and a very thick mist, the whole area was engulfed and visibility was almost nil. We just looked into the distance in disbelief, and as we wound our way down the paths the mist became thicker and thicker, and the rain heavier and heavier. What a letdown, there was nothing to be seen except the signpost pointing to different corners of the world. So here we were, 11 January, 2012, on the northern most tip of the North Island after visiting the southernmost tip of the South Island on 30 November, 2011 .... 42 days to zig-zag our way from the south to the north of New Zealand, approximately 2,061 kilometres, what a disappointment!

Decision time once again. What would we do? Kiss the earth and say we've been there and done that, or, find somewhere to stay overnight and hope for better weather the next morning. We'd found quite early on in our travels in New Zealand it could pour with rain one day and be beautiful the next. There wasn't a hook up site in this locality for some 60 kilometres, back down the road we'd just travelled. But, hey, hang on! Our conservation campsite (DoC) booklet came in handy once again, and we found a lovely site a couple of kilometres from Cape Reigna, down a gravel track, right beside the beach at Spirit's Bay!

The rain was lashing down and poor little Isaac's wipers were fighting, yet again, but he was winning the battle. Even though we could hear the sea crashing and splashing onto the shore and the rocks, we couldn't see anything at all. We just hoped we hadn't parked actually on the shore or on the top of a sandbank!

In the darkness and the stillness that surrounded us, we cooked a meal and bedded down for the night. Hoping none of the Maori Spirits would be leaping into the ocean and disturbing our sleep, otherwise we might have found ourselves hurtling back up the road, in terror. We could hear the pitter patter of rain on the roof of the van, and the occasional swoosh as the Pacific Ocean as it lapped against the shore line, but otherwise there was silence. It was pitch black outside, and we had only seen the lights of two other vans arrive earlier in the evening.

Bill amused himself and tried to frighten me by saying, "Ooo! What's that out there? Oh, it's ok it's just the spirits walking along the beach!"

As he fell asleep, after totally winding me up, all I could hear were his gentle snores rising above the pattering rain and the gentle lapping of the sea. I suddenly felt quite alone, and probably heard more noises than were actually out there. I put my head under the duvet and I was off to sleep, eventually!

By morning the rain had stopped and the sun was shining onto the beautiful sandy beach. We'd survived the night and so we sat drinking our early morning mug of tea and gazed out to the horizon. It was a wonderful uplifting place with only a couple of other camper vans having braved the night. Thank goodness it had been a quiet night, no leaping of spirits, or if they had, they were considerate and leapt very quietly.

The sun had certainly got its hat on so we had a rather hurried breakfast, alfresco of course, and being a day behind with our expected journeying time we would do a quick clean up, zoom back up to Cape Reigna, a quick viewing and back on the road. Only I just couldn't resist a paddle along the seashore before we left, it was gorgeous. I watched as Bill began to pack the van, and then I furtively nipped off, over the small mound of grass and onto the beach. With sandals in hand I wandered along the shoreline, aimlessly splashing in the small ripples of the waves, whilst watching the odd cloud float across the blue skies and wishing it farewell. Though, a cheeky monkey had suspected my antics, and unbeknown to me had followed me onto the beach, armed with my camera, what a nerve, he got all the evidence he needed as he caught me slacking! Imagine the scene, we probably looked quite manic, with me running along the beach and Bill chasing me, and at the same time he clicked and clicked the camera. He wasn't content with one photograph for evidence, he got a whole handful.

All packed up we set off back up the hill to Cape Reigna, parked up, and back onto the pathways down to the lighthouse with the signpost stating it was only 18,029 kilometres to London. What a difference a day makes! The views were spectacular, as the waves of the Tasman Sea met the swirling currents of the Pacific Ocean. The two seas were battling against each other. It was an amazing sight. Although no matter how hard we tried, with binoculars and camera, we couldn't even make out a silhouette of the Three King Islands, but we were more than happy with our morning viewing, absolutely fantastic. So, farewell to the leaping spirits and we're on the road again.

"♪Do do de da. We're on the road again. Do de da da♪."

Oh well, you know what they say if you can't beat them just join in! As I started to sing along, Bill stopped singing and gave me a very, 'that's my song,' look.

I just had to laugh!

Chapter 10

The Treaty of Waitangi

It was Friday, 13 January and we had travelled down from Cape Reigna to the Bay of Islands and our next port of call was Kerikeri.

Kerikeri is a sub-tropical paradise and the largest town in the Northland. It was also called 'the cradle of the nation,' being the site of the first permanent "mission station" in the country, and had some of the most historic buildings in New Zealand. The Mission House can still be seen and is the oldest wooden structure still standing, it now belongs to the New Zealand Historic Places Trust. It was built by the Church Missionary Society for Rev. John Butler who was New Zealand's first Western Clergyman.

We arrived at the Kerikeri Top Ten Holiday Park, which was in a peaceful country setting, yet only minutes from the town. It was a tranquil site with a river running along the bottom park where visitors were able to canoe or swim. It was idyllic just sitting watching the activities, the children jumping in the river with squeals of delight as they thrashed about in the water, but looking very cold as they emerged onto the river bank.

We spent the Saturday morning catching up on housekeeping. Didn't take long with our little van though, but then, there was always the clothes washing to catch up with, especially as we got so very wet again at Cape Reigna. In the afternoon we strolled up town, which was just about a five-minute walk and noticed the film 'The Iron Lady' was showing at the cinema. We booked a cinema/meal deal for that evening and had a good evening out.

On the Sunday morning, we met two local Quakers at the small Meeting of the Bay of Islands and worshipped with them along with two visitors. We enjoyed a shared lunch after which we presented the Quaker story to the two ladies.

It was a lovely afternoon and they said, "We'd lifted their spirit," by worshipping with them and showing them the history of Quakerism. Their response exhilarated us as they were very genuine and it was all so worthwhile. Afterwards, with hugs and goodbyes we wished our two hosts well and travelled on to Pahia. We booked into the Waitangi Holiday Park in Paihia as we intended to visit the Treaty House in Waitangi the next morning.

With an early start in the morning, we crossed the bridge on foot over the Waitangi River on our way to the Treaty House situated in the Waitangi Treaty Grounds, which is set in the Waitangi National Trust Estate comprising of 506 hectares of grounds.

Rich in resources the Bay of Islands attracted early Polynesian Settlers and was occupied by competing Maori tribes. In the late 18th century, European explorers Cook and Du Fresne, visited the Bay. Whalers, sealers and traders set up bases there and Christian Mission stations were established at Rangihua (1815), Kerikeri (1819) and Paihia (1823). Trade muskets made international wars deadlier and by 1830 the Bay was crowded with visiting ships. The trading centre at Kororareka (Russell) had an unsavoury reputation as the 'Hell-hole of the Pacific.' Disturbed by reports of lawless behavior the British government appointed James Busby as British Resident in New Zealand.

Busby arrived in Paihia in 1833 and settled in Waitangi. Without resources to enforce his authority Busby was described by Maori as 'a man-o-war without guns,' but he did useful work as a mediator. In 1834, he helped northern chiefs obtain a maritime flag and registrations for locally built ships. In 1835, he hosted a gathering of 35 Northern chiefs who signed the Declaration of Independence of New Zealand

The Treaty of Waitangi – 1840

In January, 1840, Captain William Hobson arrived in the Bay of Islands to make a treaty with the Maori chiefs on behalf of the British Government, Busby helped revise Hobson's draft and Rev. Henry Williams of Paihia and his son Edmond, translated it into Maori.

On 5 February, 1840, hundreds of Maori and scores of Europeans gathered in front of the Residency of Waitangi. The Treaty was read and explained in English and Maori. The Chiefs debated all day at Waitangi and into the night at Te Tii, across the river. On the 6 February, 43 Chiefs signed the Treaty in front of the Residency at Waitangi. Copies of the Treaty were then carried around the country. Hobson claimed British Sovereignty over the whole country on 21 May, 1840. By September 1840, over 500 Chiefs had signed the Treaty.

Though debate continues over the interpretation of some of its parts, the Treaty is best understood as a whole. It is an agreement between two peoples to live and work together in one nation. This agreement is as relevant today as in 1840, for it guarantees the rights of both Maori and non-Maori citizens in Aotearoa, New Zealand.

The Treaty of Waitangi

HER MAJESTY, Victoria, Queen of the United Kingdom of Great Britain and Ireland, regarding with Her Royal Favour the Native Chiefs and Tribes of New Zealand, and anxious to protect their just Rights and Property, and to secure to them the enjoyment of Peace and Good Order, has deemed it necessary, in consequence of the great number of Her Majesty's Subjects who have already settled in New Zealand, and the rapid extension of Emigration both from Europe and Australia which is still in progress, to constitute and appoint a functionary properly authorized to treat with the Aborigines of New Zealand for the recognition of Her Majesty's Sovereign authority over the whole or by part of these islands. Her Majesty, therefore, being desirous to establish a settled form of Civil Government with a view to avert the evil consequences which must result from the absence of the necessary Laws and Institutions alike to the Native population and to Her Subjects, had been graciously pleased to empower and authorize me, WILLIAM HOBSON, a Captain in Her Majesty's Royal Navy, Consul, and Lieutenant-Governor of such parts of New Zealand as may be, or hereafter shall be, ceded to Her Majesty, to invite the confederated and independent Chiefs of New Zealand to concur in the following Articles and Conditions.

ARTICLE THE FIRST

The Chiefs of the Confederation of the United Tribes of New Zealand, and the separate and independent Chiefs who have now become members of the Confederation, cede to Her Majesty the Queen of England, absolutely and without reservation, all the rights and powers of Sovereignty which the said Confederation or Individual Chiefs respectively exercise or possess, or may be supposed to exercise or to possess, over their respective Territories as the sole Sovereigns thereof.

ARTICLE THE SECOND

Her Majesty the Queen of England confirms and guarantees to the Chiefs and Tribes of New Zealand, and to the respective families and individuals thereof, the full, exclusive, and undisturbed possession of their Lands and Estates, Forests, Fisheries, and other properties which they may collectively or individually possess, so long as it is their wish and desire to retain the same in their possession; but the Chiefs of the United Tribes, and the Individual Chiefs yield to Her Majesty the exclusive right of Pre-emption over such lands as the proprietors thereof may be disposed to alienate, at such prices as may be agreed upon between the respective proprietors and persons appointed by Her Majesty to treat with them in that behalf.

ARTICLE THE THIRD

In consideration thereof, Her Majesty the Queen of England extends to the Natives of New Zealand, being assembled in Congress, at Victoria, in Waitangi, and We, the Separate and Independent Chiefs of New Zealand, claiming authority of the Tribes and Territories which are specified after our respective names, having been made fully to understand the Provision of the foregoing Treaty, accept and enter into the same in the full spirit and meaning thereof, in witness of which, we have attached our signatures or marks at the places and dates respectively specified.

Done at Waitangi, this sixth day of February in the year of Our Lord one thousand and eight hundred and forty.

W. HOBSON, Lieutenant-Governor

The above is the English version and there has been controversy over the translation.

The second and third articles have caused controversy through the years, mainly because of translation problems. Successive governments believed the Treaty enabled complete sovereignty over Maori, their lands and resources. The Maori believed that they were merely giving permission for the British to use their land.

From "Souvenir Guide, Waitangi Treaty Grounds"

At Hobson's Beach the Waka House shelters the 35-metre-long 'Ngatokimatawhaorua', a minimum of seventy-six paddlers were required to handle it safely on the water. This massive waka was launched as part of the Centenary Celebration in 1940 and was made from three kauri trees felled in the Puketi Forest. It is a larger version of the normal waka. This was part of the 20th century work by the Maoris to revitalize their cultural claim to equal partnership in the Treaty, and the ceremonial use of the Treaty Grounds in the future.

We toured the Treaty House, an absolutely fascinating building, which had been restored to its original condition as far as was possible. In the parlour of the Treaty House there was a figure of the British resident James Busby.

In 1844 Busby sailed to the USA to sell kauri gum. However, whilst he was away war broke out between some Northern Maori chiefs and the government. His wife, Agnes, and their children left for Sydney. The cedar windows and doors were removed from the house to Paihia for safekeeping. War parties stripped lead from the roof and the British Army camped in the house and grounds. Repairs were eventually made to the house and new wings added after the Busby family returned in 1846.

Ten years after the death of James Busby his widow and children sold the house and the surrounding estate. Over the next fifty or so years the house was neglected, renovated and neglected again. Finally, in 1933 it underwent major restoration work and was named 'The Treaty House' and yet more restoration work was seen in 1990.

Te Whare Runanga

This Maori Meeting House stands alongside the Treaty House and was opened during the Treaty Centenary Celebrations. It symbolizes

Maori involvement in the signing of the Treaty. Te Whare Runanga is a typical meeting house in appearance, but is unique in that it was planned to be shared by all Maori tribes. It is a national Marae Meeting House, as distinct from a tribal one.

In typical colonial style the Treaty was used one sided by the British for many years. It is only recently that this has been recognized and the Maoris and the New Zealand government have been negotiating to bring a better balance to the relationship between them, and for compensating action recognizing Maori legitimate claims under the Treaty.

We had an excellent day at the Waitangi Treaty Grounds as well as lunch in the café. Well worth a visit, such important foundational history for New Zealand.

www.waitangi.net.nz

Whangerei Water Falls

We were back onto State Highway 1 the next morning, as we journeyed down to Whangerei. We had planned to stay overnight at the Whangerei Falls Holiday Park, partly as this was a good stop off on the way back down to Takapuna, and it was also within walking distance of the falls. This holiday park was lovely with a hot tub and a swimming pool. The hot tub definitely had our names on it.

We later walked to the falls and took some splendid snaps. The waterfalls in New Zealand are plentiful and bountiful, so peaceful and relaxing sitting by them, as they were rarely crowded, in fact, we seldom saw anyone at all. We then followed the footpaths to the A H Reid Memorial Kauri Park, this park is a remnant of the original kauri forests, which were once extensive throughout the Northland. It's named after A H Reed, a New Zealand Historian, author, (he wrote 'The Story of Early Dunedin' in 1956) publisher and long distance walker, whose homestead was on the other side of the river and the upper car park.

The walk between the waterfalls and the park follows the Hatea River and has lots of places to swim or picnic along the way. We soon came to the sinuous canopy boardwalk, high across the creek, where we walked between 500-year-old kauri trees. It was quite a wonderful walk and seeing the kauri trees, once again, was a real bonus. We'd become kauri fans, magnificent trees and beautiful wood. We didn't have much time left as evening drew to a close, so we didn't have the opportunity to explore the town of Whangerei. We always seemed to get so wrapped up in the nature and history of this incredible country, wherever our journeying took us.

Mr Nippy Tail makes an appearance.

The following morning, we continued our journey heading towards Takapuna, over the bay north of Auckland and to one of our favourite campsites. We'd planned to call in to visit another isolated Quaker at Ruakaka, who due to ill health hadn't been able to attend a Meeting for Worship. Although, some from the meeting did try to visit her whenever possible. Bill made contact and they invited us to call in for lunch, which considering we hadn't met them before was a lovely gesture. After lunch, we were given a whistle stop tour of the area. Our hosts pointed out the landmarks and told us how the area had changed so much, as industry had become a big part of the scenery.

After the tour, they invited us back to their home for a cup of tea, big smile on Bill's face now, and a look around their lovely garden. We were standing under the canopy on their decking, sipping tea and chatting. Bill and I were recounting the tale of the illusive Australian White Spotted Tailed Spider, they stood with mouths open, aghast. They were quite shocked and said how strange as they had never seen one. At this point I just happened to look up, and I was off the decking like a shot. As there, hanging underneath the canopy and looking down on us was the culprit, or one of his family, who had quite probably followed us all around the North Island! (And then down came the spider and sat down beside her.) Not a chance. I was off. We couldn't believe it. It was an Australian White Spotted Tailed Spider. I kid you not. Obviously, it had been listening to our sorry tale. Well the commotion began, I squealed, Bill jumped, our hosts jumped and the men whacked and whacked it. No more hitching rides on the back of our van. Our hosts must have been mortified and probably spent the rest of the day stripping the canopy and decking to try to find Mr Nippy Tail's family. What a tale they would have to tell!

Fond farewells and a big 'thank you' for a lovely day, and an apology if we had left Mr Nippy Tail's family with them. What lovely people. We left feeling so blessed and ready for the next leg of our journey. Hopefully, without any of Mr Nippy Tail's relatives.

Takapuna, North Shore and a Scottish castle

It was the middle of January and the weather was still quite hot but thankfully without the rain. We detoured on the way to Takapuna and hooked up at the lovely little resort of Waipu Cove. It's a small village with a golden sandy beach around an enclosed bay. The campsite was next to the sea front, so we had a lovely walk around the bay in the evening. We then sat in silence, watching the sunset over the horizon, and as the sun was about to disappear Bill jumped with delight, and I just about fell off my seat. The silence and the moment were gone, as Bill jumped around, he had espied a kingfisher.

"Did you see that?" he yelled. "The kingfisher was waving at me."

"No Bill, he was flapping his wings in readiness for take-off!"

The following morning, we drove back to State Highway 1 on course for Takapuna. On the way, we called into the small town of Kawakawa, for a loo stop, and what a surprise that was. It resembled the main street of a Western movie, with a steam powered locomotive running down the middle of the street.

Were we glad that we needed a loo stop, because this wasn't just 'any old toilet' it was something I'd never seen before, but Bill knew it straight away.

"Ahh! Hundertwasser," was all Bill said, rather reverently.

I didn't get it and replied, "What does it matter? I just need to spend a penny."

There on the main street, was the work of art created by the reclusive Friedrich Hundertwasser in 1997. He was an Austrian painter, architect, ecologist and philosopher and had made his home in Kawakawa from 1975 until his death in 2000. It was the only project he had completed in the southern hemisphere, and it was his last. It was constructed completely with recycled materials; including spent glass bottles, bricks, broken tiles, mosaics, small sculptures, coloured glass, and a living tree intergrated into the design. It was an indulgent re-cycled paradise 'Hundertwasser' style.

Bill insisted on taking photographs of the inside and outside, hard luck if there was anyone in there. Bill was in his element. You see he is the 'Greenman' and is insatiable about re-cycling. In fact, I'd often been heard to say, "Don't stand still for too long or Bill may well recycle you." We were so lucky to fall upon this interesting creation.

We drove back onto State Highway 1 and headed down to Takapuna, no stops on the way, it would have been so tempting to try to take in every tourist sight, but our schedule was becoming tighter and tighter. We travelled through the valleys of Wayby and Dome amid the dense green forests. The hillsides were a mass of very dark green trees going up and up almost to the top. It's something I'd never noticed before, even in England. I think the intensity of the dark green, against the brilliance of the azure blueness of the sky, made them stand out all the more. The landscapes in New Zealand just tumbled and rolled, and there was something different around every corner.

We arrived at Takapuna, a northern suburb of Auckland, it was a lovely vibrant city and quite trendy, with bars, restaurants, cafes and boutique shops. We soon found our way to the Takapuna Holiday Park. Oh, we do like our beachfronts! It was a superb location overlooking Rangitoto Island and panoramic views of the beautiful Hauraki Gulf.

Ah! What a relief it was to hook up, put the kettle on, get the chairs out and soak up the view with all the sailing boats heading north from Auckland (we were approximately 10 – 15 kilometres from Auckland city centre). This, amazingly, was the first time we had seen people walk on water! We may have been a bit behind with the times but that's literally what it looked like. Yes, you got it, they were standing on boards with a paddle. These boarders looked very relaxed as they indulged in the tranquility of gliding along the vibrant blue water, and didn't seem at all perplexed that they may fall off. I think I was more concerned than they were.

The following afternoon we'd decided to do the Takapuna Milford Walk with a very helpful pamphlet from the site office. The walk was mainly along public roads, with paths and highlights of facts about some of the historical buildings in the area. Part of the route followed the foreshore, so it was advisable to go at low tide. Some of it crossed private property, which I found slightly daunting, as I wasn't quite sure whether or not we were following the correct route.

Bill, being very gung-ho just kept saying, "Come on, no one's going to shoot you."

"Really?"

The walk is known locally as Takapuna's Golden Mile, with much of its historic architecture, flora and geology being well preserved. Apparently, in the early days the areas around Takapuna, Milford Beaches and Lake Pupuke were where the wealthy Auckland businessmen built homes for their families. The houses were usually second homes, but for some they became their permanent residence, so popular was this part of the coastline. Takapuna and Milford Beaches had also been places for day trippers, arriving on the Devonport Steamer Ferry, the visitors would step straight onto the beach at Takapuna.

We walked the Takapuna Milford Walk guided by a booklet produced by the North Shore City Council and saw Algie's castle (real name Merkesworth Castle). Captain John Alexander Algie had built a house in the shape of a castle to remind him of his homeland of Scotland. There was the Circle/Goldie House, a circular apartment building with 360° views. There were the Sea Walls and the Giant's Chair, which had the same theme as Algie's castle. And finally, the Fossil Forest where a volcano had erupted and covered the forest with hot lava. At low tide, there were approximately 500 burnt out tree stumps on the shore. There were many other interesting buildings on the walk, it was a lovely way to spend the afternoon.

The reason we were there was to meet up with Christine and Pauline, my cousins, which was emotional and wonderful at the same time. We spent most of Saturday together and were wined and dined at Christine's lovely friend's house just near the beach. On the Sunday, we gathered with the family for a special lunch to celebrate Aunty Betty's eightieth birthday. It was amazing to meet my Kiwi family and we had a very pleasant gathering at The Falls Hotel. I never thought I would be doing this journey; it hadn't been on my radar at all. What a marvelous experience, but an absolute tremendous bonus to meet up with family members, whom I hadn't seen for over fifty years.

We joined the Takapuna Quaker Meeting on the Sunday morning, where we shared worship with them and later told them of our journey and news from Christchurch. They were enthused about our visit, and said they would love to see the Quaker story presentation. So, we booked a date and would return to Takapuna.

Chapter 11

An Unexpected Journey

Coromandel Peninsula
It hadn't been our intention to drive up the Coromandel Peninsula, as time was rushing on, and we still had so much travelling to do and people to meet. But on good advice from some local Kiwis (people not birds), we decided to give it a quick tour. Oh boy, we weren't disappointed. This peninsula is a holiday destination for many New Zealanders, where they spend time fishing, swimming or simply relaxing. It had a very balmy climate, and was approximately 85 kilometres long jutting out into the sea between the Hauraki Gulf and the Pacific Ocean. The Coromandel Range was sculpted by volcanic activity, as is a lot of New Zealand. It was very steep and hilly and largely covered by temperate rain forest (Coromandel Park Forest), which occupied much of the centre. Due to the nature of this leg of land most of the Peninsula's population was in clusters in a small number of towns and communities around the coast. The area was largely known for its hard rock gold mining and the kauri tree industry.

Our first port of call was to be Thames, (weren't we here on Boxing Day? Ouch!), on the west coast and the gateway to the Coromandel Peninsula. It had originally been two towns, Grahamstown and Shortland. We hooked up at the Dickson Holiday Park which was an ideal first base for our journey up the Peninsula. It was in a lovely tranquil park setting with mature trees and sheltered sites. As we parked the van we would always look to see where the sun was, to get the best of the day and to eat alfresco. However, this caused quite a lot of confusion to begin with, as the compass points are in the opposite direction in the UK. We conversed just about daily, as to which was east, which was west, or maybe just permanent confusion for me, being such a poor navigator.

I was just about always wrong! The park had a lovely butterfly garden, which we visited the next morning before leaving the site. Absolutely fascinating seeing tropical butterflies flying around. How beautiful all the different species were, with their deep blue, orange, turquoise and green wings.

So, we were off on our whistle stop tour of the Coromandel Peninsula hoping it wouldn't push us too far out of our schedule.

"What schedule?" asked Bill,

"Ah! you see it's all in my head," I replied.

I caught a glimpse of a look of panic on his face.

We travelled up the west coast of the Peninsula on a beautiful stretch of winding road, up and up with such spectacular scenery all the way. The pohutukawa trees were plentiful in this area, and were still in colour with a blaze of red flowers. The scenery flashed past us as we drove up and down these twisty, twining roads, and caught glimpses of sand and turquoise, transparent, crystal clear waters. After what seemed like a very long and hot journey, in fact only approximately 58 kilometres, we arrived at Coromandel town. The main road being through the centre of the town, as with so many in New Zealand, was lined with shops, cafes, art stores, pottery stores and much more.

A gold strike in the 1860s saw the population dramatically rise to 10,000. Coromandel is the northern most town of any substance on this peninsula. The name Coromandel being taken from the British Royal Navy supply ship 'Coromandel', which visited the harbour in 1820 to collect kauri.

Apparently, in the 1960/70s property prices were very low due to the declining industry in this former gold town. But the closeness of the bush, beaches and hills enticed hippies, artists and new-agers. It's an area plentiful with artists, crafters, healing centres and organic market gardens.

We drove through the town and onto Rings Road where we would stay at the Coromandel Holiday Park. Later we walked into the town to stock up on supplies and to have a meander around. We stopped at a little café for a pot of tea, they were advertising for a WWOOFer (a voluntary position where you work in exchange for a bed for the night and food).

I offered Bills services but they said, "No, he was too hairy!"
www.wwoof.co.nz
Live and learn the organic way.
Connecting hosts and volunteers organically.

Whitianga

We left the next morning to travel to Whitianga, approximately 46 kilometres away, it would have been indulgent to travel to the furthest point on this scenic peninsula to Fletcher Bay or Port Charles, but unfortunately time was against us.

We discussed this at length but subsequently as I pointed out to Bill, "We were after all, somewhere we didn't intend to be."

We set off to cross the mountains to Whitianga. There was no easy access, we had to drive on State Highway 25 up to Kuaotunu and then down the highway to Whitianga. The only other alternative was the route 309 road, which was a 22-kilometre-long unsealed (gravel) road and considered extremely dangerous, so we stuck to the main road. After all, it wouldn't have been too good for poor old Isaac either. We arrived around lunchtime and found Whitianga to be a pretty town overlooking the Mecury Bay. We hooked up for the night here, as we intended to visit Hot Water Beach on the way back down the Peninsula. Bill thought we would spend the afternoon lazing and reading on the Hot Water beach sands, but you know what thought did? He didn't know I had a little surprise in store for him.

Hot Water Beach

It was Wednesday, 25 January, and we were due back in Takapuna on the Saturday to prepare to deliver our Quaker Story to the Takapuna Meeting on the Sunday. Dumped and topped up with water we headed off down State Highway 25 to Hot Water Beach. I don't know why, but I really didn't believe we'd be able to dig a hole in the sand and bathe in hot water. Well there I go again, 'doubting Sylvia'.

We left State Highway 25 at Whenuakite and veered off onto Hot Water Beach Road. Like most beaches in New Zealand it wasn't very busy, initially. There was a shop on the edge of the car park just before the beach where you could buy or hire a spade to dig your hole, but I'd thought of this beforehand and didn't feel it warranted a full-size spade. Whilst in Coromandel I had bought a child's spade for each of us, a green one for Bill, and a pink one for me, or was it the other way around? Pleased with myself, I thought I'd surprise Bill, so after we'd parked up on the beach car park I produced the two spades. They weren't really small children's spades, they were big spades for children. Bill's face became distorted and his nostrils flared slightly as his face contorted into an absolute picture of disgust. Oh dear!

"What am I supposed to do with that?" He said most indignantly, as he eyed other people walking past our van with their great big shovels.

"Dig," I said, "prove there's hot water under the sand."

Bill looked even more exasperated as a big strapping lad with a very big spade walked past, with a very big smile on his face, whilst looking at Bill and his spade.

Bill pushed his green spade back into my hand and said, "Ok, but you carry it until we get onto the beach, and make sure we go somewhere quiet, I don't want to be seen with a child's spade."

Quiet it couldn't have been much quieter. So, happily, with my two spades, one pink and one green, I headed along the beach, I was quite proud of my little finds. Surprisingly, no one was digging so we wandered around a little. Then quite suddenly, as the sea began to ebb, and just about out of nowhere, groups of people appeared and went and stood at the tide line with their very big spades and shovels. As we watched the water slowly retreat groups of people started to dig. The beach began to fill up, and as they dug others started to gather around jostling for position, as though they were digging for gold. We stood quite a way back from them by a very large rock, as they dug and dug. Much to my amusement Bill still wasn't taking ownership of his lovely green spade. Suddenly, we realized our feet were sinking into the sand in the very shallow water, as the tide ebbed out towards the horizon.

Bill wriggled his feet in even deeper and jumped as he said, "Ouch, that's warm, in fact that's hot!"

Yep, we'd found a hot patch. Very quietly, and watching the other groups intently, we began to dig. Not too fervently, as we didn't want to draw attention to our little patch, and our little spades. I think it was at this point that Bill fell in love with his little green spade, as by this time he wouldn't part with it at all. He was like a little rabbit burrowing for its life. As we dug, the hole began to fill with water and became warmer and warmer.

Some children from the large group, that were digging further along the beach, came running over to us.

"Have you found hot water?" they asked.

Oh dear!

"No, no," we replied, and I could see our noses growing longer by the minute. All our hard work with our little spades, we wanted the first dip. An Australian couple arrived and stood watching us, they looked very amused at two poms digging with children's little/big spades. We quietly told them of our discovery and invited them into our hot water pool. It was amazing, it was getting hotter and hotter.

Oh no, I remembered my camera was in the van. Although how I was going to prove it really was hot water with a photograph, I would never know.

On my return, Bill was surrounded by children wanting to dip into our pool, he kept shooing them away, "No, no hot water here."

Meanwhile, the groups further along the beach were still digging, with their big shovels and spades. We were laughing with a sense of achievement as we related our story of our two 'little/big spades' to the Australian couple, and how Bill had felt silly with a child's spade. We all had a good tee hee hee, and a hot bath. We then felt mean so we invited the children to bathe in our newfound spa. Talk about ownership. Soon and to our astonishment the water became so hot that you couldn't even dip your toe into it. The funniest sight was that of Bill "ouch, ouching," his way out of the pool and hopping about on one foot. Well, I thought it was hilarious. Although, I did get a long stare when I asked him if it was a bit too hot. We then found ourselves standing guard and warning the children not to go near it and so to pacify them we gave them our magic 'little/big spades' and suggested they go dig another hole. Well, box ticked we said our goodbyes to our new-found friends and headed back to the van, and, on the road again.

We then spent the next hour or so very animatedly chatting and giggling about how good our spades were, and marveling at discovering our own little spa pool.

Bill actually succumbed and said, "That was very clever of you buying those brilliant little spades before we arrived, what a lovely surprise." I rest my case. Nothing to do with luck of course! Sometimes small is good enough.

We were heading back to Miranda for a couple of nights to catch up on the housekeeping, before going back to Takapuna. Bill also had a yen to do some more sea bird watching on the shores and visit the coastal bird centre. We arrived at Miranda early evening and were quite tired, such a lot of digging in the afternoon, and it had been quite hard work renting out our spa pool, as everyone kept haggling about the price!

Chapter 12

Heading to Paradise

Takapuna and Clarks Beach

On the Saturday, we left Miranda and headed back to Takapuna to settle onto one of our favourite sites right on the sea front. Unfortunately, we couldn't get a plot overlooking the sea, but it was still lovely and we were able to walk down onto the beach from the van.

On Sunday, 29 January we made our way to the Hearing Centre where Takapuna Quakers held their Meeting for Worship. We had a problem though, we couldn't gain access into the building. We were to attend Meeting for Worship and afterwards present the Quaker story. The gate that was usually open was locked and even going through the library, which was part of the same building as the centre, we couldn't gain access. We enquired at the desk in the library and they sent security to try and help us find a way in. Some Friends from Auckland arrived as they wanted to join us and lend support to Takapuna Meeting. We all became exasperated as it soon became a comedy of errors. Two of us going up and down in the lift, with no success. The security guard by then was quite red in the face and not at all amused, as he tried the fire escapes and every door on the way up. Whilst the three from Auckland went up and down the stairs trying any doors they came across. What a fiasco it was. Time was moving on and we were already late for Meeting for Worship. Whatever would they think of us? Finally, our friends from Auckland found a way in, but then they had to try and round the rest of us up. Bill had wandered off in another direction. Talk about the blind leading the blind in the deaf centre!

Well, eventually we made it. Although I don't know about the security guard, as he was last seen running up and down the fire escapes. Oh dear, maybe he's still there or spending the rest of his days looking for two strange poms who sent him on a wild goose chase!

After Meeting for Worship and a lovely shared lunch we delivered our presentation and had a brief discussion and question time. Everyone said they had enjoyed it immensely. Though I did wonder if we'd been locked out deliberately, as when we mentioned that we'd been unable to gain entry there were a few smiles and "Oh! how strange." They didn't seem too concerned!

We'd made the decision to leave the city for a couple of nights before taking the ferry to Waiheke Island, which had been highly recommended to us as a must do by the resident Friends in Auckland. We drove for about 40 minutes south of Auckland down the west coast (our east coast), I was still very confused about east and west. We eventually found Clarks Beach Holiday Park, which was very nice but very busy and quite noisy. The owner had a tractor and trailer and spent some of his time ferrying children around the park. Although later, we were rather disappointed, as this was the first time we had really noisy neighbours playing very loud, not our type, of music. The sort of stuff that just seems to bang, bang, boom.

To top it all, the owner of the site came along and said, "There's a disco tonight, why don't you come along and join in you'll be made very welcome?" ARGHHHH! Oh dear, we'd found the crazy, loud, young part of New Zealand, it was like being in another country. What? Grey gappers discoing! I don't think so. I did ask our neighbours if they would turn the music down a tad and a rather big strapping young man obliged, but then the females in the party objected and it was turned back up even louder, so much for a peaceful evening. Thankfully the majority of them left the next morning, so we smiled and waved them goodbye and had a lovely quiet afternoon and evening.

Paradise on Waiheke Island

On Tuesday, 31 January we took the ferry from Half Moon Bay, Auckland to Waiheke Island where there was a Quaker retreat house. Ginna and Davie recommended the island as an absolute must. They suggested it would be a good break for us, before we were to return to Auckland and cover for them for two weeks at the Centre. We couldn't resist, booked five nights on Waiheke Island and hoped the weather would hold.

Waiheke Island

The earliest known settler to Waiheke can trace their ancestry back to the Tainui canoe that landed at Onetangi and gave the island its first name, Te Motu Aria Roa, meaning the long sheltering island. One of the first settlers to reach Waiheke was Samuel Marsden, who preached there in 1818 and established a mission near Matiatia. Again, the same cycle seems to have been used through the years, of kauri logging, gum digging and clearance for farming. Eventually the Victorians found a love for the magnificent coastal scenery on the island. They flooded over in boats full, to picnic and probably bathe in the beautiful turquoise waters. As access from Auckland became much simpler and quicker, and the fact that land on the island, among some dramatic landscapes, was relatively cheap it drew people to move onto it, especially artists and craft people.

The ferry from Half Moon Bay to Waiheke Island was for small vehicles and foot passengers, it was quite busy. It was a short journey and the ferries ran quite frequently. It was well used, as some people lived on the Island but would commute to work in the city of Auckland. How idyllic to arrive home to such a beautiful, much slower pace of life.

We arrived at the harbour of Matiatia around mid-afternoon, after an easy sail across the Tamaki Strait. Our journey to Palm Beach was quite straightforward and in no time at all we had arrived for our mini break. Here it was, we had found a paradise in the Hauraki Gulf about 17 kilometres from Auckland. Friends House on Waiheke Island is a Quaker Meeting House/Retreat built on the hillside overlooking Palm Beach. The views were magnificent across the Hauraki Gulf towards the tip of the Coromandel Peninsula and the Little Great Barrier Islands. There was decking around the front and sides of the house, enabling us to sit and look over the ocean waves towards the horizon.

The house had been built by voluntary labour in the late 1980s and was run on a non-profit basis, whilst volunteers helped to maintain the building and the grounds. A retreat for Quakers and attenders wanting peaceful, inspiring surroundings in which to relax, reflect, and discover the important things in life. The house was spacious inside and had been constructed with groups in mind. However, we had a lovely double bedroom, quite a luxury for us, and the use of the lounge and kitchen. Perfect to unwind after all the travelling and dusty roads.

We spent the first day relaxing, catching up on housekeeping and looking around the small community. We had a walk along Palm Beach. We were going to take a footpath up and over the cliffs along the coastline to the next small town, but then I realized the next beach was a nudist beach. Oh dear, I just couldn't or wouldn't. Poor Bill, he wanted a walk and was so intent on marching across the beach and up the cliffs with or without me, until we espied a small group of children who were literally hanging out of the branches of a tree, giggling and pulling faces. We were curious, then we realised that the branches of the tree overlooked the nudist beach, which was very well hidden, so by climbing the tree the children would get an exceptionally good view across to the 'forbidden' beach. Bill changed his mind and we would retreat to our retreat.

As we walked back up Palm Beach we heard some shouting. Suddenly the children ran past us squealing. Running as fast as they could, whilst kicking up sand with their flip flops as they went. On looking back to see what had caused the commotion, there in a small gap in the rocks beside the tree, was a very irate, red-faced, elderly man with a hat over a certain part of his body, yelling at the children. We both burst out laughing and hurried along the beach at a quick pace, in fact almost as fast as the children.

The next morning, we caught a bus to Onerawa, a small town up the coast. It's a settlement spread across a small isthmus between Oneroa Bay and Blackpool Beach. There were some lovely shops and cafes so we had a walk around and became very adventurous stopping for a couple of beers and a bowl of chips, how exciting!

World War II Tunnels

On the Friday, we drove up the island to Stony Batter Historic reserve, which is a maze of World War II tunnels on the eastern tip of the Island. It was built in 1941 to defend Auckland harbour during World War II and can be found a twenty-minute walk over private farmland from the car park on Man O' War Bay Road. Stony Batter is a web of hand-dug tunnels, which took us about an hour to explore. You needed a torch, as it was pitch black in the tunnels, but we discovered we could have hired torches on the site. There was also an interesting hilltop counter bombardment battery. We were given a map of the tunnels and Bill was in his element, back to the seven-year-old planning the battle. It didn't take long before we lost each other or I lost Bill, as he does tend to wander off and do his own thing. I found it quite scary wandering around on my own as I seemed to be going around in circles. Then the horrible thought crossed my mind, would he notice once he got back to the van that I was lost, or would he take great delight in driving off without me for a few days' peace and quiet. Mmmm! Worrying. I eventually found Bill and wasn't surprised to see him on the hilltop counter bombardment battery – I thought someone else was with him, but I was wrong. He was busy talking to himself and having his own little battle. What did I say about the seven-year-old?

We agreed to disband our armies and go see the lady who sold us the tickets and see if she could offer a cup of tea or some such refreshment, but there was something very strange that made us feel uneasy. We made a hasty retreat and back up the road to the safety of little Isaac.

On the Saturday, we strolled along the beach watching everyone enjoy their time in the sea and playing on the sand. We decided to sit down and enjoy the beauty around us, while we listened to the waves crashing onto the golden sands. We heard some laughter and then squealing. Looking up we saw a not so young looking woman, lying on a surf board, bobbing up and down on the waves and then falling off, which caused much hilarity from those around her.

We looked at each other and Bill said, "Can't be much fun she's just yelling and squealing all the time."

Well, I thought, how silly to put yourself through that, what fun could it be? Silly woman.

So off we went to find the little French man selling crepes, (French Pancakes) at the side of Palm Beach. We'd seen him earlier and couldn't resist, they were gorgeous. Fairly sated, we plodded back up the beach to the house and spent the evening preparing for Meeting for Worship the next morning.

We had a very spiritual Meeting for Worship on the Sunday morning and a lovely shared lunch with local Friends. We then told the George Fox story through our 1652 Quaker presentation and had a lovely chat afterwards.

Bodyboarding on Paradise

As the sun had become quite hot later in the afternoon, we thought it would be nice to spend our last day, on this beautiful island, on the beach. Off I went to get my cosie, towel etc., but when Bill re-appeared he had two surf boards under his arm.

"You really think I'm going to make a fool of myself and do that surfing stuff? Not a chance." I said, as I glared at the boards.

Once down on the beach Bill went into the sea with one of the boards, and I thought, gosh I'll never live this down if I don't at least try. With much trepidation, I followed Bill into the sea, board under my arm, and trying to look as though I'd been surfing all my life. Two very young boys and four older boys suddenly appeared beside us in the sea. Oh dear! Oh well, I thought, in for a penny in for a pound, we're leaving tomorrow so no one will see us again. Off we trudged into the lion's den (sea) and threw ourselves onto our boards as the waves leapt up and came crashing back down. Wow, exhilarating, fun, and yes, we wanted more. So back we went time and again. As the waves became bigger we watched the youngsters and tried to copy them. The boys were all in competition to see who could ride the wave the furthest and we soon found ourselves trying to compete too. Oh, what fun! We laughed and giggled as the waves whacked us off the boards and we went under. At one point, we were laughing so much that the youngsters were quite put off and kept falling off their boards, which made us laugh even more. Looking up the beach, I realized there were quite a few people pointing and laughing, in fact some were in absolute fits of laughter, though surely not at us? Well, it must have looked a sight to see two grey gappers trying to compete with these young athletic boys. This thought threw me into a fit of hysterics. I then fell off and got a big mouthful of seawater, so after much coughing and spluttering I decided to call it a day. Later in our journey, we said we'd been surfing on Palm Beach to which we were told, "No, just body boarding!" Oh well, it was as good as a surf to us.

It was soon Monday morning and with sadness and a fond farewell to Paradise, we made our way back to the ferry, and on to Auckland for our stint as relief Voluntary Resident Friends at the Auckland centre and Meeting House. It had been quite difficult re-packing the van for our onward journey, as we both had sore ribs and aching stomach muscles, but hadn't a clue why? It must have been some of the gardening we'd been doing!

Chapter 13

Two Cities on the North Island

Auckland

We arrived back in Auckland on Monday, 6 February after our wonderful rest on Waiheke Island. We were to look after the Quaker centre whilst Ginna and Davie had a break and a well-earned rest. There was a two-night overlap, to cover some of the procedures before we took over the helm. We had another tour of the buildings and rooms. We were to sleep in their bedroom whilst they were away, so we could let the other rooms, if possible. Friends centre in Auckland offers a very relaxing and friendly bed and breakfast service to Quakers and attenders.

Unfortunately, before our hosts left, the centre was burgled. It happened at about 1 o'clock in the morning. The burglars entered via the resident friend's bedroom window and took some personal items and a laptop. It appeared they had also, as it became apparent sometime later, wandered through the rest of the rooms in the centre. The Resident Friends awoke and actually saw the burglars leave their bedroom. It was terrifying for them when they realised someone had been roaming around the place whilst they slept. Unwanted company in the dead of the night.

We joined them for breakfast the next morning and were shocked to learn of the incident. We hadn't heard a peep, as we'd been sleeping in the annexe at the back of the centre. We hadn't even heard the police arrive or any noise at all. I did feel rather guilty that we'd slept right through it all, and hadn't been there to support them. They were probably thinking, oh great, we're going away and these two will sleep through anything.

They left on the Wednesday to take what was by then, a more than well-deserved break. It had been a very traumatic experience for them, they were both quite shaken.

We took extra great care to lock up, and have a good look around the gardens and the outside buildings to ensure everything was secure in the evenings. I was quite surprised I didn't feel afraid really. We wanted Ginna and Davie to have a very restful break, so we just got on with it. Before they left, we suggested that they should take a few extra days and go to 'paradise', Waiheke Island, where else? After all they'd introduced us to it. We took over our duties and got on with our own chores. Bill enjoyed a really good 'fix' of gardening as he pruned, weeded, and cut the grass. I did our usual catch up on housekeeping, clothes washing and a general clear out of the van along with the running of the centre.

We joined in with some local Quaker activities and got to know local Friends as we had a couple of walks with them. One was to Judges Bay and another to an old water reservoir which had been transformed into a lovely parkland with waterfowl.

We presented our Quaker Story to the Auckland Local Meeting on the Sunday, with Bill's new, we didn't know how to use projector, (that was fun), and later enjoyed a shared lunch.

On the Monday, it thundered with the usual 'Pacific' downpour, oh well we were in the tropics after all! Although, as in the tropics, it soon cleared. So, with brollies in hand, just in case there was another downpour, we went for a walk and climbed up the paths from Mount Eden Road to the top of Mount Eden. Mount Eden is Auckland's highest volcanic crater at about 196 metres, it's one of the many volcanic craters jutting up out of the relatively flat land of the city and suburbs around. It had been made into parkland and was classed as a sacred place for local Maori. It was a fairly steep climb up, but the paths were solid and easy to walk. We were quite surprised when we got to the top to look down into the crater, it wasn't huge but very impressive. It was all grassed over with ropes and signs to keep people out of it. The views from the top were stunning right across the city. We could see other mounds pushing up out of the suburbs of Auckland. In the distance was the Sky tower, some 328 metres high, New Zealand's tallest structure and just bigger than the Eiffel Tower and Sydney's Centre point. It had observation decks, with views over the city and the Hauraki Gulf and a revolving restaurant, which was highly recommended to us. Unfortunately, we didn't have the opportunity to visit the Sky Tower, as time and finances weren't on our side, but never say never!

As we walked around the top of Mount Eden we saw some small birds flitting here and there, in and out of the shrubs and long grasses. Bill was in his element, another bird to add to his collection. I just sort of hung around as Bill kept whizzing past me with binoculars in hand, and at the same time only just avoiding knocking over anyone who got in his way, whilst he tried to identify this tiny bird.

"Job done," he stated, "definitely a juvenile goldcrest."

I whole-heartedly agreed with him. "Absolutely, yes, it is. Now shall we move on," as I pushed him towards the next path and away from the birds. Lo' and behold here we go again as we moved further around and into an area surrounded by Pine trees he espied a Parrot. Ok, Bill - parrot, parrot - Bill, and who was chasing who? I really didn't know. But I did manage to get a good shot of it as quickly as I possibly could, as the cacophonic noise of its screams and squawks and at times sloppy kissing sounds, were penetrating my ears. I managed to persuade Bill the photograph would be good enough to identify the parrot by looking in the bird book back at the van. It turned out to be an eastern estrella another introduction from Australia, but at least this Australian didn't bite, or it may have done if Bill had continued with the chase!

On the Wednesday evening, we had supper at my cousin Christine's home, which was lovely. She lives in Torbay, North Shore, and took us on a trip to the farm where she used to work and live. It was wonderful with open countryside swathing down to the beaches. She told us stories of how her family and friends would go camping on the beach to celebrate New Year's Eve, partying, barbequing and swimming. What a fantastic way to bring in the New Year, but not possible in our back yard in Britain I'm afraid.

On the Thursday evening, we paid a visit to Galbraiths Ale House on Mount Eden Road. It was a character building and was once the Grafton Public Library. What a fascinating pub. The beer was brewed on site and we watched it bubbling and frothing from a viewing area. It was renowned to be one of the best places in New Zealand to drink craft beer, and they reckoned they could trace the origin of every pint.

As we entered Galbraiths the aroma of the hops and brewing enveloped us. It's a pub in a brewery and a brewery in a pub. The main public room was big and airy, just off this was a long thin room with individual shaped sofa seats down one wall. The opposite wall was glass and this was where the brewery vats were. We sat and watched as one of the big vats frothed so much it lifted the lid off, the froth then poured down the sides leaving a stronger smell of hops. We were quite transfixed watching it bubble and froth whilst Bill enjoyed a glass of Munich Lager. As they say in the Ale House 'No tricks or gimmicks just honest beer.'

We were due to leave Auckland on the Saturday, we'd already stayed longer than we had anticipated, but then Ginna and Davie took us up on the offer of an extra few days in paradise, on Waiheke Island. We were so pleased they'd taken this opportunity, as they arrived back looking so much more relaxed and ready for their next stint at the centre. On the Friday, we planned another visit to my Aunty Betty. We had lunch with her and a very enjoyable and informative chat about family. Later in the day we said a very tearful farewell, but I couldn't face telling her we would be travelling south and probably not see her again. It was actually very upsetting.

Hamilton

Well, stint done in Auckland, we were on the road and heading down the North Island to Hamilton. Ah! I had forgotten how peaceful it was when Bill didn't sing. I should have held that thought, as it didn't take long for me to remember how annoying it was when it all began again.

"On the road again, di di do do da."

We travelled on State Highway 1, past Drury, where we'd brought the New Year in at the Quaker Summer Gathering. It was about 125 kilometres to Hamilton so we pulled off at Te Kauwhata having completed the largest part of the journey and had a picnic by Lake Waikare. It was a beautiful place with picnic benches, grassed areas and tremendous scenery. We had a leisurely cup of tea and some quiet time. It was so peaceful and rejuvenating.

We arrived in Hamilton City in the late afternoon, we soon found the Hamilton City holiday park, with its beautiful park like gardens. It was very spacious and only about two kilometres from the city centre. Hamilton is on the banks of the river Waikato and is New Zealand's fourth largest city. It isn't a major tourist destination but worth a visit for it's beautiful gardens.

The site was quite close to the university campus where the Quaker Meeting for Worship would be held the next morning. We hooked up for the night and had a walk around the immediate area to get our bearings for the next day, Sunday, and Meeting for Worship. We woke up the next morning to brilliant sunshine and initially debated whether we should walk or drive to Meeting for Worship. Then we discussed the fact that we could easily lose our way, especially if I had the map! We really didn't want to be so dreadfully late, as we were touting our presentation for a few weeks hence, and it would be so awful to tumble into the Meeting half way through.

We had a lovely peaceful Meeting and a chat with local Friends and booked a date for the presentation, so Bill was dancing with joy. How he loved to get lost in his own little world. He would transport his audience along with him, as they became transfixed listening and watching the power point presentation. However, more often than not, he would go off on a tangent talking about something else, his audiences' eyes would begin to glaze over and he would then say with that little lost boy look, "Where was I?" I would then bring him closely back to heel!

We looked around Hamilton in the afternoon. We were delighted we had as it was the Hamilton Garden Festival. The gardens were huge and it was very busy with all sorts of activities and lots of families milling around. The gardens were themed with Italian, Indian, American, English, Maori, Japanese Garden of Contemplation, Chinese, Kitchen, each had its own authentic theme and was really well nurtured and cared for. There were walkways and footpaths along the river, a café, a restaurant and an information centre. The facilities were very good. February is the time of year for the Summer Garden festival; yes, I know it's odd, late summer in February? There was dancing, shows and games for the children, and adults if they wanted to participate. We couldn't see all of the themed gardens as some of were being used as mini theatres and workshops. We could easily have spent a full day in there, as it was so beautifully tended and inspiring.

After a splendid afternoon, full of colour, with the smell of beautiful roses, and the sight of the rhododendrons cascading over the lawns; the sound of laughter and children running around with blobs of ice cream on their noses; and that wonderful big yellow thing glowing in the sky, we felt very relaxed as we returned to Isaac. We cooked a meal and prepared to depart the next morning for Rotorua the land of thermals. (Volcanic not underwear!)

Chapter 14

Steam Valley

Thermal Rotorua and a Maori Experience
It was about 110 kilometres from Hamilton to Rotorua so we had quite a leisurely journey on State Highway 1 and then joined State Highway 5 at Tirau. Rotorua is in the main active geo-thermal area of New Zealand, situated on the southern shores of Lake Rotorua, and is one of the biggest tourist attractions on the North Island. We could smell the town long before we could see it, as the smell of sulphur pervaded the air. As we drove closer and closer the stench of rotten eggs became stronger and stronger.

We chose to stay at the Rotorua Thermal Holiday Park as it had free thermal pools, which we just couldn't resist. First things first though, we hooked up, sorted the van, found our bearings, and then straight into the pools. It was about 40° as we sat in the pool and mellowed. After about twenty minutes or so I could feel the tension disappearing as I started to feel quite floppy. The recommended time was no more than 25 minutes per session, but it would have been tempting to ignore this and float around in the pool to the point of looking like a shriveled prune. When the picture of a prune came to my mind I thought better of staying in any longer.

After our evening meal, we walked into the town. Along the way, we saw steam rising from the ground, through holes, and small vents. It lingered around and then disappeared into the air. The smell of sulphur was in our nostrils and hanging all around us, like something menacing. There was a large pond/small lake, I'd never seen anything like the steam that was rising from it. It was a boiling cauldron, and had quite high fences all around, with a warning sign *Danger Thermal Area.* Apparently, some people had fallen into these, and had been killed, boiled or scalded alive. It just didn't bare thinking about, how horrific!

As we drew closer to the town, the steam continued to emerge and spiralled up from cracks and crevices, floating around the shrubs and trees. It played havoc with our conscious minds, it seemed inconceivable, beyond the imagination. I couldn't get my head around it. I felt that at any moment there could be a massive bang, and an enormous geyser would erupt from middle earth, incredible.

The next morning, we visited the Rotorua Museum of Art and History, where we experienced a very good overview of the volcanic environment and the Maori culture. The museum was housed in an old bathhouse, built in 1908, and was quite ostentatious looking, with its long walkway up to it. It was originally built as a state of the art spa, using the thermal mineral waters and mud to treat people with various complaints, and conditions of any description. It was hoped to draw wealthy Europeans from across the world, but it didn't do so, and consequently had to be scaled back and suffered through lack of maintenance and investment. It was an interesting story in itself and all documented in the museum buildings. As we peered into the rooms, we saw behind the scenes, and how it had all supposedly worked. Some of the treatments were quite archaic and intrusive. It made me shiver to think about it. No, I'm not going into detail! We saw the old baths, which were quite gloomy and had the original green and white tiles and exposed pipes.

There was a display with the description of how the eruption of Mount Tarawera, in June 1886, had destroyed the Pink and White Terraces. The terraces had been a massive tourist attraction in their day, with people travelling from all over the world to see what had become known as the 'Eighth Wonder of the World'. They were situated at the north end of Lake Rotomahan and visitors journeyed by horse and carriage from Rotorua. The terraces had been formed by water containing silica cascading from boiling geysers down the hillside, as the water cooled it became crystallised, and left pools where people would bathe. The eruption had been heard quite clearly as far away as Blenheim on the South Island. Sheet lightening flashed across the sky, as the three peaks of Mount Tarawera exploded throwing hot ash and lava down the mountainside. It destroyed many Maori villages, settlers' farms and settlements, along with the Pink and White terraces, and took approximately 150 lives.

Some eleven days before the eruption, a boatful of visitors had claimed to have seen a war canoe approach their boat, only to disappear into the mist. A Maori priest in the boat claimed it was a spirit canoe, and was an omen that a great tragedy would strike.

The Eruption of Mount Tarawera

"We have passed a fearful night here the earth having been in a continual quake since midnight. At ten past two in the morning, there was a heavy quake, then a fearful roar which made everyone run out of their houses, and a grand but yet terrible sight presented itself. Mount Tarawera, close to Rotomahana, became suddenly an active volcano, belching out fire and lava to a great height. The eruption appears to have extended to several places southwards. A dense mass of ashes came pouring down and were accompanied by a suffocating smell. An immense black cloud, which extended in line from Taheke to Paeroa mountain, was one continual mass of electricity all night and is still the same. Judging from the quantities of dust here it is feared the results will be serious to the people at Wairoa and the natives around Tarawera Lake. Hundreds of new boiling springs have broken out all round here, some in the middle of the road'

From 'The New Zealand Chronicle' June 1886, collector's edition:

The museum had a docudrama film lasting about 20 minutes, it was truly shattering to watch. The seats in the little house, where the film was being shown, were quite comfy and solid until the eruption started on the screen. The seats then began to move and literally bounce up and down, so we had to hang on just to stay put. What an experience. My bums never been the same since! We were taken completely by surprise as the seats started to buck and bang, and just when we thought it had stopped it began again, it continued for quite a few minutes. Talk about being caught unawares. This gave us a very small insight as to how violent it must have been at the time of the eruption but obviously, nowhere near, not even probably remotely close to the real thing. The rest of the museum had an incredible amount of information about the Maori culture and their day-to-day lives. We saw another short film about the Second World War Maori regiment who fought in Crete, North Africa and Italy with great distinction and loss of life, many of whom were under age.

As we left the museum and made our way back to the van, we still found it amazing, in fact just quite mind blowing, as we walked through the town and the shores of Lake Rotorua. Steam was spewing from every orifice on the roads, the waysides and the foot paths, as well as from around bushes and shrubbery.

On our final evening in Rotorua we joined a tourist Maori Entertainment Evening. It was an evening of traditional Maori challenge, with welcome and dancing, as well as food and wine. They gave us an explanation of their language, tools and weapons and how the challenge and welcome are part of their culture, so as to make sure newcomers were coming in peace rather than war.

We enjoyed a "hangi" (earth oven) meal, the kai (food) was cooked in a big hole, dug on top of a thermal uprising and was steamed for something like one to four hours. It was very, very busy with many people enjoying the event. After the meal, we took a short-guided bush walk in the dark, along good paths, to see glowworms in their natural habitat and to search for kiwi birds, which were in captivity, in large enclosures. Kiwis are the native, flightless, nocturnal birds of New Zealand. When we did manage to see one, we were surprised at its size and how fast it ran back into the bush within the enclosures.

Rere atu taku manu, ka hoki mai anõ

Go forth my treasured bird, return again in your own time.

All in all, a memorable evening, ending a memorable stay in Rotorua.

Omokoroa Beach and Tauranga

It was Thursday, 23 February and we were on our way to see my cousin Pauline and her husband Bruce, who'd just moved onto a fruit farm near Tauranga. They had invited us to stay for a few days, and Christine, my cousin from North Shore, would join us at the weekend. We were really looking forward to spending some quality time with them and seeing where they lived.

On the way, we decided to stay at the Omokoroa Thermal Holiday Park. Oh dear! We just couldn't stay away from those thermal pools. It was a delightful place for an overnight stop and was, as we had come to expect in New Zealand, extremely well kept and functional. Yes, of course, even though the weather was pretty grim with a very cloudy sky and small rain showers, we still enjoyed a dip in the outdoor pool. It was lovely and refreshing.

Omokoroa is a small urban area in the Western Bay of Plenty and is considered to be part of Greater Tauranga. This small peninsula used to be a Maori area, but an early missionary settler bought it from a local Maori chief. It then became a farming community, famous for its milk products, which were sold in the developing city of Tauranga. In the 1960s it became a fruit growing area with small fruit farms emerging. The climate in this and the wider area is ideal for growing fruit, one of the main crops being kiwi fruit. Omokoroa started as a small rural holiday village, but had recently expanded to a commuter town. The expansion of feeder roads made it a little more than a 15-minute drive to Tauranga city. Some of the fruit farms are now giving way to housing and the peninsula is one of the fastest growing housing development areas in the district.

We left the next morning to make our way to Pauline and Bruce's place. They hadn't been in the house long so they were busy renovating and redecorating, as well as organizing the fruit farm. We just hoped we wouldn't be in the way, and hopefully, could help where at all possible. Christine was due to arrive later in the day, so we were to spend the weekend, chatting and walking the area of fields and fruit farms and share good food and wine. Although, the work was going to wait until Monday. They lived on the outskirts of Tauranga in a small district called Pahoia, which we had great difficulty finding. Guess who was navigating?

In the end, I had to ring Pauline, "Where are you?"

We had driven past the road end at least twice! We changed over, I drove and Bill navigated, what a team. We eventually managed to find them. Oh, what a beautiful place, secluded and sat up on the hillside over-looking the bay towards Matakana Island.

On the Saturday, we had a walk through the fields to a waterfall and along the river. Of course, the boys and the dogs couldn't resist a dip in the water, so in they went. The boys in their undies and the dogs just as they were. Boys will be boys! The water looked very inviting, but it wasn't for us girls as we watched the boys shiver.

We laughed and caught up with each other's lives. How differently we had grown up. They'd had a wonderful childhood full of barbeques, beaches, sailing, and the great outdoors. It had all been a big part of their early years and still was. Though they'd been sad, as they had longed to have family around them to share those years. As we walked back through the fields we passed through a neighbouring farm, where there were rows upon rows of kiwi fruit growing, it was an amazing sight. It would have been very tempting to pick some, especially as earlier in our travels we'd bought some golden kiwi, which we'd never tasted before, and found them to be much sweeter than the green kiwi.

On the Sunday morning Bill and I went to Tauranga and to the Quaker Meeting for Worship. We had arranged to give a talk and show our presentation. It was lovely with quite a few new people attending. There were some excellent spiritual questions and attempted answers afterwards, opening up parts of the Quaker history that the presentation had touched upon.

After a fantastic, if not emotional weekend we said goodbye to Christine, as she left to go back home to Torbay. We stayed on to help as best we could. Bill was in his element with another gardening fix, he even got to cut the grass on the ride on mower. Some people just have all the fun. Meanwhile, with paintbrush in hand, I helped indoors to catch up with some of the decorating. We had a belated Christmas meal, well we just had to, what else were Bill and I going to do with the 20 or so crackers we had left from Christmas. What a joyous and loving time we had with my fantastic Kiwi family.

All too soon it was time to say goodbye, it was difficult as the thought crossed my mind that I probably wouldn't see them again. I had so enjoyed meeting up with them and chatting about the last 50 years. It was unfortunate that we hadn't caught up before, but we'd all been busy with our families and working lives. I will never forget how welcome they made us feel and what great fun my lovely cousins were.

We headed on to Waihi Beach, which Pauline had recommended to us. We stayed at the Top Ten Holiday Park, which had really good facilities including a swimming pool and was also right across the road from the beach. In fact, the park had a small number of sites actually on the beach. The sandy beach stretched for miles, and was known to be one of the safest in the country. The next day we had a pleasant walk along the beach and found a small café, so we stopped for a pot of tea and one of New Zealand's massive sausage rolls. We had discovered these earlier in our travels and when we say they were big, they were big! We only ever needed to order one sausage roll between the two of us, as one was more than enough. We returned to the park later in the afternoon, had a dip in the pool, a relaxing BBQ, a beer and then did the usual van stuff ready to hit the road the next morning.

Chapter 15

The Garden City via Hobbiton

On the road again, and it was Saturday, 25 February and back onto State Highway 26 to Hamilton. We were due to present the 1652 Quaker story after Meeting for Worship and a shared lunch on the Sunday. By this time, Bill's rendition of the song, "♪We're on the road again♪," was becoming slightly more bearable, although I think I had learnt to switch off. I would bet by now even you've started to sing it!

Hobbiton
We seemed to have zig zagged our way up and down the North Island. This hadn't been our intention as we were conscious of the mileage we were clocking up, but it had been the only way we could fit in some of the dates and bookings. On the way across to Hamilton, we took a de-tour down State Highway 27 to Matamata, then down to Hinuera and off onto Buckland Road and there it was Hobbiton! Bill could hardly contain himself. It had been one of the sets from The Lord of the Rings Trilogy films and as we later learned was to be one of the sets for the new film The Hobbit. Bill being a massive fan of Tolkien and the Shires (Middle Earth), was just about bouncing around with excitement, no, he actually was bouncing around. There was no way we would have missed the opportunity to tour the film set.

When we arrived, we were surprised to see just a farm and farm buildings by the roadside with the Shires rest café and a small animal farmyard. We couldn't actually see anything of Hobbiton. Then we realised, it's not going to be right on the roadside for everyone to just look over a wall and say, "Oh yes there's Hobbiton, good, off we go now." No, it was very well hidden across the fields and over the hills. So, we joined the guided tour bus and were driven through the

1,250-acre sheep farm with spectacular views across to the Kaimai Ranges.

And so, the story goes; the film makers had been touring New Zealand looking for the ideal set – with no features of the 20th century. In September 1998 Peter Jackson and New Line Cinema discovered the Alexander farm during an aerial search for a suitable location. What they saw was beautiful rolling countryside with fantastic views, and as close a resemblance as they were going to get to Tolkein's Middle Earth. With the permission of the Alexander family they constructed the set for The Lord of the Rings trilogy. It was an incredible project involving a big workforce. Throughout construction and filming the site was kept under strict security due to commercial restraints by the film company.

We were told by the guide how lucky we had been to be able to tour this site, as earlier, after The Lord of the Rings had been filmed, it had been due to be dismantled. However, bad weather prevented the job being completed. This was fortunate as it had allowed the set to be re-built to film The Hobbit.

We saw the Hobbit homes, with their different shaped and coloured doors, blue, green, yellow, red. I was disappointed as I opened a door and peered in, I'd expected to see the inside furnished with little tables and chairs, and pots and pans like proper little homes. But alas no, there was nothing in them, in fact the doors were purely the frontage and that was it. No Wendy house there for me then! The inside scenes were apparently shot in studios in Wellington, but I was still very impressed with the whole set up. The Green Dragon Inn, the mill, the double arched bridge and the party tree (which had false leaves but still looked very realistic). Everything seemed so authentic and I wanted to open doors and go in or walk across the bridge, but we couldn't. I could envisage Gandalf walking across the bridge, up the hillside and along the paths to the Hobbit homes, looking for Frodo Baggins. What a wonderful experience! We were really looking forward to seeing the movie The Hobbit, as we'd been there and done that. Wow! The Green-Hobbit-man (Bill) was in his glory and shot off here and there taking photographs with my old camera, which he had somehow managed to acquire. I still wonder how that had happened?

There were other film sets from 'The Lord of the Rings' scattered around New Zealand but, unfortunately, time restrained us from visiting those.
www.hobbitontours.com

Hamilton

After our exciting visit to Hobbiton we drove up to Hamilton, to once again visit the Quaker Meeting on the Sunday, and show our Quaker history presentation. We preferred to use the same campsites at the places we revisited, especially if we found a good one. We certainly found the site in Hamilton to be acceptable with its open space and park like setting, although sometimes the unexpected happens. On the Sunday morning, I was showering in the ladies' block and was in a bit of a rush. When I stepped out of the shower, towel around me thank goodness, there was this man brushing his teeth at the sink.

He was muttering something and I just said, "Oh really." He stopped brushing his teeth and looked up into the mirror, he could obviously see me in the reflection.

He spun round, looked at me, and said, "Oh shit it's the ladies', isn't it?" Proceeded to give me a disgusting look, as though it was me that was in the wrong place, and marched out of the building with toothpaste dripping down his chin and onto his jumper. Oh and of course me, being me, where some females may have screamed with the shock of seeing a male there, I just burst out laughing. I couldn't help myself he looked so disgruntled. I then had to take control, as I would have looked quite crazy to any other females entering the block, stood there, with just a towel wrapped around me, laughing quite hysterically. Although I soon stopped laughing, as the thought entered my head, that it could be me in the wrong block. I dried off, dressed and made a hasty retreat, just in case.

We had a lovely meeting with Hamilton Friends once again, and a successful presentation. We later re-visited the Hamilton International Gardens. It was a lot quieter this time and we were able to see a lot more of the gardens, which was very relaxing. We were really glad to have had the opportunity to tour the gardens again, as this time they were all open to the public. They were excellent, and for the first time we were able to see the Chinese garden, which was well laid out and conducive to thoughtfulness, which was the original intention way back in Chinese history. As the river Waikato, ran alongside the gardens we had a stroll along the riverbank and came across the garden cemetery, which Bill went off to explore. There were interesting headstones for ex- WW I soldiers who had survived the war and died locally. It was noticeable that many of them died in their 40s and 50s and it begs the question did the war experience wear them out and cause them to die earlier than they would have?

Chapter 16

Lake, Thermal Steam and Raging River

Tirau a Corrugated Town
We said goodbye to Hamilton and travelled back down State Highway 1, we had planned to stay at Lake Taupo, one of our must-see destinations. On the way, we drove through the small town of Tirau, set in the Waikato area, amongst some of New Zealand's most fertile farmland. We'd only been on the road for about an hour but we opted to do a tea and loo break in Tirau. What a lovely surprise this little town was. On the outskirts of the town there was a big corrugated warehouse with signage that stated they could make anything in corrugated iron, as we were soon to find out. When we actually arrived in the town it was evident that this was the towns claim to fame and rightly so. They had used corrugated iron sheets, in a fascinating way, to change the shape and appearance of the buildings and decorate them, in part to show what they were selling.

There were lots of cafés, art galleries, craft shops etc. The Tourist Information Centre was situated in a large corrugated iron dog and alongside this was a corrugated iron sheep, which incorporated the Big Sheep Wool Gallery.

We had been thinking of looking to buy some small gifts to send home to our families, and this vibrant little town seemed the ideal place, with its quaint individually styled shops. We trawled the streets not just once, but twice, and were fascinated with the goods for sale. We bought some wooden postcards. We were tickled pink with these and proceeded to send them home just as they were. When weeks later they hadn't arrived, we thought we probably should have sent them in envelopes! Poor postie in Britain would be thinking, what on earth is this? Or maybe they had been challenged in customs!

There was a lovely Jade and Paua shell shop, which also sold other gifts. Unfortunately, as sometimes happens, we managed to spend quite a few dollars. Well done Tirau, you were distinctly different and certainly managed to attract us and empty our pockets.

The Jade or Greenstone is known to New Zealanders as Pounamu and has a treasured spiritual significance with its strength, durability and beauty. Originally it was used by the Maori for weapons, tools and ornamental purposes, and also was a mark of status.

The Paua Shell was treasured by the early Maori and was known as 'the Gift of the God of the Sea', with its beautiful glistening and shimmering shades of blue, green and purple hues.

On the way out of the town, we saw a sign for a Castle, Bill whooped with delight and nearly caused me to crash into a lamppost. However, it wasn't to be as 'Castle Pamela' was closed. It was only open for school holidays, statuary holidays or by appointment. It housed New Zealand's largest collection of dolls, toys and trains. Bill really spat his dummy out. He was so disappointed. He loves castles, but I couldn't understand him wanting to see the collection of dolls!

To save the day, a little further out of the town, we came across a little gem on Rotorua Road, 'The Tirau Museum'. It was privately owned. It was quirky and expansive with a collection of furniture, clocks, lamps, household articles, tobacco and honey tins, bottles, crockery, tools, heaters, radios, farm machinery, horse drawn vehicles and World War 1 and II roll of honour boards, as well as Waikato military memorabilia, guns and some fantastic classic cars and so the collection went on, and on. It was fascinating wandering around this rather dated collection of buildings with such an incredible range of historic items and machinery. We met the owner, Geoff, who had been collecting for years and had travelled the length and breadth of New Zealand and Australia looking for items to add to his collection. I think it had probably been something that had just got out of hand and so he opened it to the public. Geoff was very welcoming. We would certainly recommend the museum as an absolute must do. www.nzmuseums.co.nz/account/3158

Lake Taupo and Flying Takeaways

We arrived at the Top Ten Holiday Park at Lake Taupo, it was quite big with plenty of cabin vacancies, as it was by this time out of season. We noticed their cabins weren't too expensive and after a quick tally up, temptation got the better of us and of course with the lure of a big bed we succumbed and booked a cabin for a couple of nights. It was a lovely park with a very large swimming pool and lovely gardens and grounds. Our cabin had rolling views across the lawns of the campsite and the distant countryside. Having stocked up earlier, we enjoyed spoiling ourselves with some Spanish Tapas and a bottle of beer on the veranda. Beautiful. As we sat there we watched as people walked past and smiled, gave us a little wave, but they almost seemed to be half laughing. It took us until the next day to realize that there was a sign just to the right of this lovely little cabin, which read 'Lusty Flats'.

Taupo was a very busy resort town and was right in the centre of the North Island, some 80 kilometres from Rotorua, and set around the northern shores of Lake Taupo, New Zealand's largest lake. There were views across the Tongariro National Park towards snowcapped volcanoes. It's through there that the Waikato river wound its way to the Tasman Sea. Lake Taupo was created when the Taupo volcano erupted spewing up rock, debris and ash, which left a huge crater, now the lake.

After a welcome rest and with the weather a little dismal, we spent a while updating the blog, as we found this difficult to do whilst on the road. It was 5 March and in Britain it would be the beginning of springtime. All the flowering bulbs would be pushing through the soil, looking fresh after a long winters sleep. Snowdrops, daffodils, crocus, forsythia, tete-a-tete, with their sharp contrast of colours would be easing away the greyness of winter. Yet, it seemed strange, as here we were in New Zealand slowly heading into autumn. It was noticeable too, as in the early evenings the air had a slightly cool breeze and the night time temperatures had begun to drop.

We visited a thermal valley which was known as the 'Ninth Wonder of the World', with its geysers, steam and mud holes. However, an energy company had tapped into the steam bearing strata, they had diverted it to steam turbines to generate electricity, this had removed some of the activity of the valley. Apparently, a lot of the geysers on other sites, which you had to pay to see, were stimulated, so they would spurt at the same time each day. How convenient! We didn't bother with those but opted for a very natural walk through the bush just outside the town of Taupo.

There were lots of steaming holes. One very big one had been named the Witch's Cauldron with its bottom out of sight and vegetation growing all around it. There was another called the Dragons Mouth and again there was vegetation all around. They were very impressive and I just couldn't believe there was so much vegetation around these boiling hot cauldrons. You'd think the vegetation would become pretty soggy with all that steam.

We headed back towards the town and found the Wairakei Tourist Park just north of Lake Taupo. The Waikato, New Zealand's longest river, makes its way north from Lake Taupo between banks a 100 metres apart. Just before the Huka Falls it enters a shallow ravine of hard volcanic rock. The once placid water rumbles and roars, as it bounces off the rocks and over the Huka Falls crashing down into a turbulent swirling pool 11 metres below. The effect is 220,000 litres of water blasting by every second. This is all set amidst the exotic native forest along the banks of the river. We walked along the pathways of the Huka Falls, which had amazing views of this massive display of water, gushing and changing colour between blues and greens. A jet boat ride could take you as near to the falls as was possible.

We later discovered the Aratiatia Rapids. Where a few times a day, a siren would sound, this was to warn anyone in the river bed below the dam to get out, as the gates were about to open. The spill gates from the dam opened at the top of the Aratiatia rapids and the narrow gorge below filled with water. The water crashed down and pounded on the rocks, causing white foam and froth to bounce around the sides of the gorge. The water surged through at 90,000 litres per second. Yet within 30 minutes of the gates closing the turbulence receded to a placid stream. The natural drop was being harnessed for environmentally, sustainable, hydroelectric power. The headwaters were being diverted through a tunnel to the power station. This could all be seen from the top of the dam or a viewing platform further along the gorge.

Aratiatia means 'Stairway of Tia". It refers to a zig-zag pattern of stakes that allow travellers to ascend a steep climb. The early Moari Tia, a high priest of the Arawa tribe, passed through the gorge on his way to discover Lake Taupo.

www.newzealand.com

We walked into the town and were astonished to see the innovation of McDonalds! We thought it was their free takeaway deliveries. We were impressed! Although all those flying takeaways wouldn't be too good for the climate!

Forget the drive-thru, why not fly-thru!

There was a decommissioned aircraft as part of the McDonalds set up and they called it an air-mazing McDonalds restaurant. The disused DC-3 plane had been sat next door to McDonalds in Taupo for the last 24 years. It had been refurbished in McDonalds colours and was being used as a restaurant seating up to about 20 people.

We enjoyed discovering Lake Taupo and the surrounding area as yet again the beauty of the countryside was intense. The rivers and lake astounded us, with crystal clear blue hues shimmering in the water, foam-laden waterfalls and the density of the dark green bush and forests along with hazy steam rising all around. Goodbye Taupo. It was lovely being there and in a comfy cabin, but we were all too soon back on the road with our ever-faithful Isaac, once again camper van style.

The Thermal Valley

We were due back in Rotorua by Saturday, 11 March so we left Lake Taupo and headed north in search of more thermal pools. We arrived in the Waikite thermal valley but hadn't really looked for anywhere to stay. As we drove around some of the twisty lanes we arrived at a small site with a lot of thermal pools. Well, what do you know, what a stroke of luck, it was just there, right in front of us. This site wasn't on our campsite map so we felt very blessed to have found it. It was about 25 minutes south of Rotorua just off State Highway 5. We looked around the site, which was quite compact and didn't have the best facilities, in fact they weren't that good at all, but we were easily swayed to stay when we saw the thermal pools. Once we realized we would have free use of the pools for the duration of our stay, it was a tradeoff well worth it.

The thermal mineral pools had continuous water in and out from their source, but were drained and re-filled every evening. There was a large swimming pool, which was warmer than the average pool of this size; two lovely sit in thermal pools one of which had a roof over it, at 37 – 39c; a larger pool heated up to 40c; two hot tubs at 37 – 39c, and a series of private spa pools costing extra to use, but in the latter, you could change the temperature to your liking.

The source of these thermal pools was - The Living Waters of the Te Manaroa Spring - the largest single source of 100% pure boiling water. The water had to be cooled somewhat before entering the spa pools. Above the pools there was an Eco-Trail of geological and botanical interest. It was an educational walk and led to the amazing Te Manaroa Spring. It was incredible to watch boiling water welling up, and spurting, fountain style, out of the pool and way up into the air.

We sat in the thermal pools and whiled away the time. Whilst gazing into the distance we could only see countryside, bush and steam. This was a place for total relaxation of the body, and thoughts of the mind. We reflected about our friends in Christchurch, whose lives were in turmoil and being turned upside down. We held them in the light in the hope that they would soon have some respite. I also thought of my Kiwi family and how different their lives had been in this upside-down world. We felt so blessed and fortunate as our journey unfolded. We had met so many lovely, friendly and interesting people. Some struggling, whilst others were getting on with their lives.

It was very quiet whilst we were there, which enabled us to move around the different pools quite freely. We were soon relaxed and floppy, although beginning to look rather like two prunes! I've never known Bill get up so early in morning, so early in fact, that he was actually sat waiting for the pools to open.

We even had a final soak on the morning before we left, as this was the only site we'd come across that had a 12 noon departure time, instead of the usual 10 a.m.

The pools were widely used by the local community and were originally set up by local farmers for the use of local people. Talk about a hidden gem! Well, we certainly enjoyed this little gem of a find. Ever so relaxing; yet ever so invigorating.

We left our wonderland of pools on the Saturday and drove up to Rotorua where two local Friends had very kindly offered us a bed for the night and a lovely meal. Meeting for Worship was to be at their house the next morning, afterwards we presented the Quaker Story and shared a delightful lunch. Again, we met some lovely, interesting people and they shared their life stories with us, which was fascinating. Such hospitality in New Zealand, it was quite humbling.

It was soon Sunday afternoon and we were leaving Rotorua, another absolute must visit place. We hadn't planned anywhere to stay for the Sunday night and as we were driving south, where else would be ideal to hook up for the night? Yep you got it. We headed straight back to Waikite Thermal Valley for one final soak. Parked up, found our cosies and off to the pools. We spent a leisurely Monday morning around the pools, and once again, I was astonished, as Bill had risen early and had paced up and down waiting for the pools to open.

Chapter 17

On Course for the Settlement

We were due to stay at the Whanganui Quaker Settlement for the weekend to attend a seminar on 'Sustainability' and had planned to arrive there on Wednesday, 14 March, so we could help the settlers prepare for the weekend ahead. We were so hooked on thermal pools, that on the way down we managed to find a site with a pool and spa a few kilometres from Tarangi just south of Taupo. The pool was open 24 hours a day and the spas, complete with bubbling button jacuzzi effect, were open from 4 p.m. to 8 p.m. It was a friendly site although a little dated and in need of some refurbishment. We were turning into a right pair of soaks, so much so, that the pools began to take precedence over all else on the sites.

Ohakune
We travelled on down to Ohakune, for a stop over the next day, before our final leg to Whanganui. We drove down State Highway 1 and onto State Highway 46 along the side of Lake Rotoaira and the Tongariro National Park, we then joined State Highway 47. The scenery along this stretch was quite magnificent with rolling hills, mixed with the sharp edges of volcanic craters, different shades of green swathed along the hillsides, and in the distance was Mount Ruapehu, home to some of New Zealand's finest ski slopes.
We arrived at Ohakune, some 35 kilometres south of the National Park, to be welcomed by a huge fibreglass carrot, we gave each other one of those puzzled looks, oh what does that mean? We later discovered that it had been placed there to remind people that Ohakune was at the heart of the nation's prime market gardening region.
The town contained chalet like lodges, winter sports shops and the usual gift and craft shops. We stayed at the Ohakune Top Ten

holiday park. I liked this small town very much, it had a lovely friendly feel to it and a good atmosphere. I spent the next morning popping in and out of shops looking at the crafts and wares. Bill had found a train museum, he loves trains and history, so this was an absolute must for him. He later came back with the story of a terrible train disaster.

Tangiwai Disaster

At 10.21 p.m. on Christmas Eve, 1953, the Wellington to Auckland night express plunged into the flooded Whangaehu river at Tangiwai, 10 kilometres west of Walouru in the central North Island. There were 258 passengers on board and 151 died, and it became New Zealand's worst railway disaster.

The place name Tangiwai, means 'weeping waters' in Maori.

Most on the train were heading home for Christmas laden with gifts for their loved ones. Those waiting at the various stations had no sense of the tragedy that was unfolding. Then on Christmas Day, the then Prime Minister Sidney Holland, announced news of the accident in a radio broadcast.

Travelling at 65 kilometres per hour, the train with its nine carriages and two vans reached the severely weakened bridge at 10.21 p.m. As the bridge buckled beneath its weight, the engine plunged into the river taking all five second class carriages with it. The force of the torrent destroyed four of the carriages and those passengers had little chance of survival.

The weather on Christmas Eve had been fine, with little recent rain, no one suspected flooding in the Whangaehu River. When a goods train crossed the bridge around 7 p.m. the river appeared normal. What transformed the situation was the collapse of the dam, which held back the crater lake of nearby Mount Ruapehu, which caused the sudden release of approximately two million cubic metres of water. A six-metre-high wave containing water, ice, mud and rocks surged, tsunami-like, down the Whangaehu River. Sometime between 10.10 p.m. and 10.15 p.m. this 'lahar' struck the concrete pylons of the Tangiwai railway bridge.

At this time, there weren't any National Rescue organisations. So, members of the Forest Service, Ministry of Works, Police, Navy personnel and groups of farmers, along with other volunteers, worked through the night at the rescue operation. The river subsided very quickly but the overnight rescue operation was still extremely dangerous, as the water was fast flowing and full of debris, oil and silt.

(Adapted from: NZ History, New Zealand History on line)

'Lahar': - A lahar looks like a mass of wet concrete and contains volcanic debris, rainwater and boulders and will flow rapidly downhill.

Sustainability at Whanganui Quaker Settlement

We reached the Settlement on the Wednesday, parked and hooked up to the electricity, as we would be staying in the van for the weekend. The settlers were busy cutting up and moving trees and trimmings, which a neighbour had cut down, to let more light into her house. The next day we helped where we could in readiness for the participants arriving to attend the first seminar of 2012, that weekend.

The settlement had independent housing and gardens for each settler, as well as several hectares of communal land and gardens. A very interesting and exciting way of community living. They had photovoltaic cells on the roof of one of the communal buildings, which was producing about 9.6 kw an hour at its best. It was doing very well generating electricity from the big nuclear power station in the sky. New Zealand Quakers were putting their money to good use and making a practical statement about climate change and resources.

We presented the Quaker Story to several of the settlers on the Thursday evening.

www.quakersettlement.co.nz

The seminar on 'Sustainability', organized by the Yearly Meeting Futures Committee, began on Friday evening and had a very full and intense programme over the weekend until Sunday afternoon. There were four main speakers:

Jeanette Fitzsimons, ex co – leader of New Zealand Green Party, who first asked,

"What are we trying to sustain?" and then answered her own question with, "An economy that serves and empowers people and protects the earth."

Excellent information and argument set the scene to understand the dire situation that humanity faces in the next few years. Jeanette said she is now campaigning so her grandchildren have a chance of living something like a reasonable life in New Zealand.

John Peet, Chair of Sustainable Aotearoa, New Zealand, gave a talk entitled 'Let's start with a Steady Economy'. "He saw the need for it straight away, not in some future time, as we needed the energy and resources to bring this about, and if it was left too late to change the economy around, it will not be possible to do so. A steady state economy gives room for growth in parts of the economy when there had been some decline in other parts, but the net effect of the economy should be steady in terms of the impacts on the environment, and should not be greater than the annual ecological output of the country, or in global terms of the worlds annual ecological output."

Good solid stuff, and it was still possible, but is any government attempting to do this? It was likely that the people will have to do it and then the government will follow. So much for leadership!

Bill Rosenburg, an Economist and Director of Policy for the Council of Trade Unions spoke about the economic system that the world's governments use, and how it is fatally flawed as it relies on growth to sustain it. Can't happen indefinitely so the end is nigh. (Repent?)

Fortunately, there was a growing body of new younger economists arguing against the system, and we can only hope they grow in numbers and help governments stuck on the old discredited system to change, or maybe it will have to be the people again!

Finally, after a somewhat gloomy assault on our moral and sense of hope, we heard from a young Friend, whom with other young people had started a movement in New Zealand called "Generation Zero". The generation who are likely to be the first to be seriously affected by the impending crash of the world's economic system as it continues to outstrip the world's ecological production by over use, year after year. He said that young people have the skill and energy to fix it, so they will. There was such an abundance of certainty to his talk and discussion, that afterwards we felt truly uplifted.

We also heard about "G Force" which stands for Grandmas, Granddads, Great Aunts and Uncles campaigning for their grandchildren's right to a future. We could both sign up for that, and it would be interesting to see if there is an equivalent in the UK.

The rest of the weekend was spent seeking areas that New Zealand Quakers could work corporately to bring about change to the state of the economy and still live by their Testimonies. These areas were refined and prioritized and then participants took on some responsibility to push them onwards within the Quaker Community.

A very full weekend and by the Sunday it had all come together. We were very impressed with the Settlement and the seminar.

Green New Zealand

New Zealand is proud of its green and clean reputation, but with a small population and quite a short history this is not surprising, though Kiwis still work hard to keep this unique environmental balance. About 30% of the power in New Zealand comes from renewable energy sources especially in the steam valleys. In work, and in play, New Zealanders are doing their utmost to minimize the impact on the environment and working hard to safe guard its landscape and wildlife. The Kiwi bird, New Zealand's' national symbol, is threatened with extinction due to predators such as feral cats and dogs; the Moa, another of the country's flightless birds, was hunted to extinction by the Maoris. However, there are plentiful sanctuaries, parks and reserves, protecting and cultivating plants and wildlife. In many parts the air is clean and fresh, as are a lot of the crystal-clear lakes and rivers, all being untainted by human hand.

Although, due to poor public transport the car ownership rates are some of the highest in the world, large amounts of second hand cars were being imported from Japan, some of which wouldn't be allowed into other countries.

New Zealand deserves a big credit as to date, they have managed to stay "Nuclear Free"

Palmerston North

Sunday afternoon and we motored down from Whanganui to Palmerston North. We had met several of Palmerston North Friends at the Summer Gathering and had arranged to deliver our presentation. Some friends from Kapiti had also wanted to see it, but unfortunately, we were by then too short on time to go over to Kapiti, so we were very grateful that they travelled over to Palmerston North. We had a wonderful evening chatting, sharing stories and showing our presentation, again what lovely people and so welcoming. I even met someone from my native area in England, small world after all!

Palmerston North is a large city and is the thriving capital of the province of Manawah. The city centre is around 'The Square' and has all the usual hustle and bustle of a busy community.

We didn't see much of the city as we had booked a small basic cabin for the two nights enabling us to give Isaac a good once over before heading down to Wellington and the Interislander ferry back to the South Island.

Chapter 18

Sailing South via the Capital City

Wellington
"♪ On the road again ♪." Oh no, I had so enjoyed the peace and quiet whilst travelling down the North Island, but no, it wasn't to be. He's at it again and still out of tune. I gripped the steering wheel even harder and gritted my teeth as we journeyed down to New Zealand's cosmopolitan and bustling capital, Wellington. We were to stay bed and breakfast with the Resident Friends at the Wellington Quaker centre.

Wellington is quite compact and nestles between the harbour and the hills in the background. Whilst there we visited the 'Te Papa Museum of New Zealand', another absolutely fascinating place of heritage and historic interest. It was a large building on the waterfront and I would say covered everything that is 'New Zealand'. It was excellent for adults and children alike and very educational. There was a level with an interactive section on earthquakes and volcanoes, where you could experience a realistic quake inside a shaking house. View displays on the fault line that ran right through Wellington, and even watch Mount Ruapehu erupt on screen. There was an outdoor bush experience, a level for the Maori story and a large display of the Treaty of Waitangi. Another level was dedicated to New Zealand's national art collection with an ever-changing display of works on paper, oils, and sculptures representing New Zealand's art world past and present. It would really be a full day to see the whole museum, but there were a couple of cafes to provide some sustenance to keep you going.

We presented the Quaker story to twenty or so people at the Wellington Meeting House, and had a lovely supper whilst we chatted with local Friends some of whom, we once again, had met at the Summer Gathering.

As it rained the whole time we were in Wellington we didn't see quite as much of the city as we would have liked to, but we did manage to get out into the neighbouring countryside for a couple of long walks in the rain, with our usual overdressed attire. Time seemed to rush past us and sadly it was soon our final departure day, and goodbye to the North Island of New Zealand.

Goodbye North Island

It was Thursday, 22 March, and we were saying our final goodbyes and taking the ferry back to the South Island. As we waited for the Interislander ferry, I had a strong feeling that I was leaving something behind. I could feel my emotions welling up. What were we leaving behind? Oh, my goodness, all the lovely people we had met, their hospitality, warmth, their friendliness and their knowledge and advice. The most spectacular, diverse and awesome Pacific Island, New Zealand's North Island. But a large part of my sorrow was leaving behind my lovely Kiwi family, whom I hadn't seen for over 50 years, yes, this brought tears to my eyes and emptiness in my heart. I hoped the emptiness would eventually be replaced with wonderful memories, as I would hold them dearly in my heart and mind forever.

We had a very good crossing and the weather was much better than when we arrived on the North Island in December. We were on the top deck for quite some time watching the island fade into the distance, and praying we would hold on to all the memories and experiences. As Wellington slowly faded into the hillside and as there wasn't much else to see in the way of sea life, we went below deck to get a drink and a bite to eat. Afterwards, I stayed below whilst Bill went back up onto the deck in search of sea life, I was catching up on some knitting, gloves for our glacier walk. Ha! I've let the cat out of the bag, that's why I was buying wool and needles in Oamaru. Bill left me with rucksacks, iPad and all the usual bundle that I tended to trail around with me, just in case I needed something, of course. Off he went looking for dolphins, whales, penguins, seals, sea lions any form of sea life. Binoculars, as usual slung over his shoulder and muttering that he hoped he would see something on this crossing. Oh dear, I hoped he would see something too!

About half an hour later the Captain announced that there was a pod of dolphins swimming alongside the ship. Everyone suddenly stopped what they were doing and hurriedly headed up to the deck. No, slight exaggeration not everyone, some just looked up and gave a sigh, they'd obviously seen it all before. Oh no! I looked around me and there was really no way I could gather everything together, and get up in time to find Bill, in case he hadn't heard the announcement. Then I thought, oh blow, why not and began to frantically pack up. Before I'd managed to pack and bundle all my - may need items - together, Bill reappeared.

He came strolling towards me with a long face and said, "Don't know what's happening, but people are charging up the stairs, maybe they're going to jump ship. Ha, silly beggars. I just can't believe I haven't seen anything again."

He then realized I was scrambling around trying to get everything piled into my two little arms and looked at me as though I had gone slightly mad.

"Go back up the stairs," I said, "at least one of us should see them. The Captain has just announced there are dolphins swimming alongside the ship."

Bill set off at a pace heading the wrong way, and so I yelled, "No, no starboard side."

As if I knew what I was talking about. When I eventually, and believe me I wasn't far behind Bill, managed to gather everything together I set off to run towards the stairs when I noticed some people, left behind below deck, were staring at me as though I was some sort of a raving lunatic. It must have been the balls of wool unraveling along the floor. I can imagine their thoughts - mad Pom. But, despite all the hassle I managed to catch a glimpse of those wonderful sea creatures, as they were playfully diving in out of the sea in the wake of the ships current. Apparently, this is known as 'riding the bow' and can save them energy, I felt so blessed, what a wonderful sight to behold.

As we left the dolphins behind I gave them a wave and I could see a big smile on their faces and a wink of their eyes. How they had enjoyed entertaining the passengers and seeing us all look on in awe, but just in a day's work to them. They probably laughed all the way back to Wellington. Bill didn't believe me that they'd smiled and winked, but it really didn't matter because I knew it was true! What an incredible never to be forgotten sight and a really lovely goodbye to the North Island. Typical of course I'd left my camera below deck with Isaac so no photos of dolphins. I couldn't believe it, what a tragedy!

Chapter 19

Mistletoe and Wine

Queen Charlotte Sound
We arrived in Picton later in the afternoon, after what had been an eventful and exciting crossing. Bill was in his element as he talked nonstop, to anyone who would listen, about how he nearly missed the dolphins. It would have been a lot quieter for us all if he had! After leaving the ferry we drove along the south side of the beautiful Queen Charlotte Sound and opted to head off to Havelock some 35 kilometres away. It took us quite a bit longer to drive along the narrow winding road to Havelock than we had expected it to, as I couldn't resist stopping to take photographs. There were such breathtaking panoramic views across the two sounds of the Queen Charlotte and the Pelorus. We booked into a small basic cabin at the Havelock Motor Camp in the historic town of Havelock, which was located at the head of the Pelorus Sound, part of the Marlborough Sounds.

We had a meal and then re-checked the map. We were due to travel down the west coast, but the scenery was so spectacular around Queen Charlotte Sound that we thought it was probably well worth a quick visit, and would squeeze in another day. This really did leave us tight for time, but again it was something not to miss and how right we were.

The next morning, we set off on our journey up the Peninsula wedged in between the Queen Charlotte Sound and the Pelorus Sound. We drove back along Queen Charlotte Drive and then headed off to the left and up Kenepuru Road, which took us along Mahau Sound and eventually to Te Mahia. It was a slow drive as the road narrowed and twisted, giving us glimpses of unbelievable views of the bays and inlets with turquoise blue waters.

We travelled onwards and upwards and at lunchtime found a small bay with a hostel/hotel that served food and drinks. It had outdoor seating with incredible views across the bay. We had a pot of tea and pizza, not too exciting but believe me if someone else is cooking it's a gourmet meal. It was such an idyllic setting, very relaxing, as we watched the small boats going to and fro. Apparently, you could catch a lift with the mail boat if you wanted to explore the bays, or there were water taxis.

We always felt as though we were rushing through this beautiful countryside, with some of the most panoramic, picturesque and photogenic landscapes, I had possibly ever seen. However, this couldn't be helped, due to our schedule of meetings and places to visit. We travelled on as far as we could to a DoC site set in a little bay. It was secluded with golden sand, hidden away by the trees and the bush. You could actually have pretended to have been Robinson Crusoe, I rather think someone thought he was! After an hour on the beach, lolling by the turquoise waters in one of the sheltered coves, we looked at the time and decided we really should make our way back down the Sound to find a stopover for the night.

Mistletoe Bay

As we were meandering back down the twisty road we saw a sign for Mistletoe Bay Eco Village, so we would go and explore. What a lovely site, actually in the bay. It was a sustainable eco village facility and we could actually camp there overlooking the bay, with views out into the sound and across the ever-changing shades of still blue water.

Mistletoe Bay Trust is a 'not for profit' organization and has created a sustainable eco village facility. The Trustees are all volunteers. The facility offers an experience that would be memorable and educational – where visitor's young and old would learn "hands on" how to live sustainably within a coastal ecosystem.

'Mistletoe Bay' showcases New Zealand's finest qualities, native bush, endemic fauna, clear water, solitude, recreation and peace. A unique place in New Zealand with an Enviro Gold 4 plus star Qualmark facility, including energy conservation.

The accommodation comprised of cabins, a cottage and camping groups were welcomed. All the accommodation was double glazed and heavily insulated with heat pumps and solar powered water heating. Water was re-cycled from a high-tech wastewater plant and used to flush all the toilets, and the rainwater was collected from all the buildings. All waste was processed and re-cycled. Mistletoe Bay was thoughtfully and deliberately placed to encourage positive, reduced-impact interaction with nature.
www.mistletoebay.co.nz

We travelled back to Blenheim on the Saturday evening to spend time with two Friends, where we had a very good evening meal and social time. It was good to hear of other people's life journeys. We had a house Meeting for Worship and presented the Quaker Story on the Sunday, with a few local friends, before moving on to Nelson on Sunday evening.

Marlborough Wine Region

The plains that lie around the town of Blenheim are famous for some of New Zealand's most prized wines. The region has a combination of cool yet high amounts of sunshine climate, usually with low rainfall and is protected by the Richmond Range. Most of the wineries offer cellar door tastings and you can usually try whichever wine you prefer.

Nelson and Rabbit Island

We joined State Highway 6 again and travelled back up to Havelock, and then along the winding road by the side of Mount Rutland and the Rui River, the scenery was as spectacular as ever. It was about 115 kilometres drive to Nelson and as it was late in the afternoon we motored on, determined to arrive in Nelson not too late in the evening. We were also heading into autumn and the nights were drawing in and becoming cooler so we wanted to get hooked up before dark. We found a campsite near the city centre of Nelson but it was quite a shaded and cold site with mainly graveled surfaces. We really wanted to find a beach setting again. The next day we moved on to Tahua Beach Camp, which was near the airport and as the weather was becoming noticeably colder opted for a cabin, which was warm and spacious compared to our little van. It was odd, almost baffling, to think that autumn was on the way yet it was only the end of March.

Nelson was a thriving small city set on the coast between the Arthur and Richmond ranges, it's one of the oldest settlements in New Zealand. It had been occupied by the Ngati Tumatakokiri people, some of whom provided a reception committee for Abel Tasman's longboats at Murderer's Bay, (now Golden Bay) where they killed four of his sailors.

The beaches were wonderful and within walking distance of our site. We spent the next couple of days catching up with the blog, doing the usual chores and shopping. We had really caught up with ourselves, as we even found some time to relax on the beach.

Being near the airport flights were crossing above us, this didn't bother either of us. In fact, I found it fascinating watching the planes flying over and wondering where they were going to or coming from. I hadn't really done this before, but I suppose being literally on the other side of the world it was beguiling, or maybe just a bout of homesickness, not necessarily for country but definitely for kin.

It was lovely to meet Quakers in Nelson and show our presentation, enjoy some food with them and chat in general. It's always good to talk to local people, even though some were from Britain, you find out lots about the area, where to visit and the do's and don'ts of the land.

Unfortunately, we both lost a tooth filling whilst in Nelson. What on earth had we been doing? A visit to a lovely dentist called Alex and all was resolved. Alex had travelled to England with his young family and was hoping to do so again. He said he'd be willing to do a house swap, but he couldn't imagine anyone wanting to visit New Zealand in the winter months. Although, Nelson is the sunniest part of the South Island and it couldn't be that bad, think of all those grape vines. It sounded plausible to me, as it would surely be better than our winters in the north of England. We left Nelson on Thursday, 29 March and were driving west to Golden Bay. We had been told of a place called Rabbit Island just outside Nelson by some of the local people, apparently, a must visit place. We looked it up on the map and found it was on our way up to Motueka.

Rabbit Island was linked to the mainland by a causeway, it was covered with pine plantations and had been set up as a public reserve. We parked up and went off to discover this lovely island. There were BBQ's, (we found that most parks and public areas had coin operated gas bbq's), picnic areas, cycle tracks, and was being used as a recreational area, although no dogs were allowed onto the island. We wandered the isolated beach with miles and miles of golden sand and the occasional drift wood display. We wished we'd found it earlier what a fantastic retreat. Rabbit Island? I don't know what happened to all the rabbits, as we didn't see any!

Chapter 20

From a Golden Bay to a Frozen Walk

We were back on the road and heading for Golden Bay and a campsite on the beach at Pohara. We did a lunch stop at Motueka. The usual, kettle on and raid the fridge.

Split Apple Rock and the Ngarua Caves
We moved on, and were on a mission to view the Split Apple Rock, a large boulder split in two that actually looks like a split apple, but we would need to find it first. It was just off Kaiteriteri Beach in shallow waters in the Tasman Bay off the northern coast of the South Island. We eventually, and I mean eventually, found the car park and had a lovely walk down a sloping track, with a wooden bridge and steps through trees and bush and onto the beach. The sand was golden and sparkling, it was a very secluded bay. And there, sitting in the waters of the Tasman Sea was the Split Apple rock, quite fascinating. It was a granite rock which possibly split when water seeped into a crack, froze and later expanded.

The Maori legend says, 'Two Maori Gods were fighting for possession of the large rock. To settle the argument, they used their - God like strength - to split it in half.'

We then drove up onto the limestone hills on State Highway 60 and followed the road leading over Takaka Hill. We had read of some caves in this area, the Ngarua Caves, and were hoping to find them before travelling onto our next destination. We found them, without much debate, our navigational skills must have improved or maybe they were just easy to find! We pulled up and made our way to the visitor centre to enquire about visiting the caves. The caves were about 20 kilometres north of Motueka and there were guided tours every hour. We booked a couple of places on the next tour and had a little walk around whilst we waited. The guide arrived and provided us with hard hats and off we went down into the darkness. The caves had electric lights, which were switched on as we went down. We marveled at the magnificent variety of stalactites and stalagmites. The lights were switched on and off as we walked through to give an ambience of the darkness, and oh yes, it was pitch black. The guide pointed out moa bones lying in the dusty sand. The moa is one of the now extinct flightless birds of New Zealand. Geologically speaking, holes had probably opened up from time to time in the cave roof. These poor flightless birds would fall through, and in the darkness, they probably wandered around, or blundered around until eventually they would have starved to death. This small site was an amazing experience, with friendly staff and a cup of tea at the end of our visit.

By mid-afternoon we had found the site at Pohara, but as it wasn't high season we thought there would probably be plenty of plots vacant so we would check in later in the afternoon. We had noticed how much quieter a lot of these sites were as we were heading into autumn and even though it was the weekend we felt certain we'd be ok to book in a little later.

Pohara and Land Slips

We continued up State Highway 60 leading to Cape Farewell and Farewell Spit. We were curious to visit this area, as we would have been here in December, if I hadn't booked us into Blenheim – and lucky I did, as they'd had a massive amount of rainfall, which in turn led to lots of flooding and landslips. This was the only road up to the uppermost northern tip of the South Island. It runs between the Kahurangi National Park on one side and the Tasman Sea on the other. It was the usual type of winding road as we climbed up and up into the hills, but suddenly, we came to halt, as the road was in such bad repair that we couldn't travel beyond Collingwood. There was evidence of landslides all along the hills. The campsite we would have stayed on in December at Port Puponga was no longer accessible as the road was impassable and closed. Wow! We were so lucky not to have been involved in all of that. With quiet humility, we turned back and headed down to Pohara and a beautiful beach setting.

At which point Bill actually took my hand and said, "Thank you for my birthday in Blenheim." He'd thanked me again? Gulp! I was filling up.

On the Sunday morning, we did the usual checks on the van, filling the water tank, dumping etc., and then travelled to Patons Rock Bay where we had a walk along the beach and lunched at leisure. It was later as we strolled along the beach again that we saw a seal, which was obviously in distress, so we waited awhile and watched. Some people walked past it, as though it didn't exist. Whilst others went towards it and seemed to try to show it the way back to the sea. But it appeared to be quite angry and just sort of half growled at them. I wanted a closer look. When I see any sort of animal in trouble my heart melts and I so want to help them, but after approaching the seal I realized there was absolutely nothing I could do. So frustrating! I didn't even know any numbers I could ring for help. I suddenly noticed Bill had wandered off, as he was prone to, and when I caught sight of him he was wading his way into the sea alongside some rocks. Oh dear, what's Bill doing now? I turned around towards the seal again and an elderly man appeared. He was walking towards the seal and getting very annoyed with it, whilst he tried to move it back to the sea. Alas, the seal was having none of it.

As I walked towards the rocks, where by that time Bill was thigh deep in water, I stopped to ask the man if he would be able to help the seal. Apparently no, they must let nature take its course. This made me feel quite sad. I felt helpless, but I suppose he was right, they know their own country and their wildlife.

As I began to walk away the man said, "I wish it would get back into the sea and die there, at least it would be food for some other creature. I'm bloody sick of burying them on the beach."

I turned and looked at him and felt a wave of nausea, I looked at the seal and felt pity. I had to get away, quickly. I was off across the sand, tears running down my cheeks. I found myself clambering over the rocks to see 'what Bills doing now?' He was on the other side of the rocks up to his chest in seawater, and so excited. I try to tell him about the seal but he wasn't listening, as he had found a bed (in the sea of course) of good-sized mussels and was busy counting his quota.

"Go get a bucket quick," he spluttered as the sea was rising to his neck. I looked back to where the seal was still lying and the man still trying to cajole it into the sea. I didn't want to have to walk past it again. I found it so upsetting. Anyway, off I went, doing as I was told for once. I collected a bucket from the van, all the time trying to avert my gaze from the seal and the man. I made it, and Bill was happy with his 49 mussels in a bucket to take to our hosts later that evening.

"Erm, why 49 Bill?" I asked. Bill gave me one of those - don't you know anything looks.

"Just in case," he replied. "Just in case I've counted wrong, I don't want to go over the quota and get arrested do I?"

"Oh!" I said, "Silly me."

The Quota for mussels was 50 per person per day and there were two of us?

Self-sufficient Friends

We were very kindly invited to stay the night with Friends Albie and Fill Burgers who have a 120-acre farm just outside Takara, in Golden Bay. They gave us a whistle stop tour of the farm, where they rear cows and sheep, and grow trees. Shortly after they moved onto the farm they realised the roof needed repairing, and even though they were fairly isolated it wasn't long before neighbours and friends gathered to lend a hand. Once the work was finished they all shared food and drinks. This seemed to be prevalent in New Zealand. We heard so many stories where neighbours and friends gathered together to help with maintenance and repairs.

Now that's what I call community spirit!

As Quakers, they were especially interested in contacting people around the world, to share ideas about world peace, bringing up children and simply getting to know people elsewhere. As well as being part-time farmers they were seeking every possible form of alternative sustainability.

Albie was spending his retirement "inventing" and building energy projects:
Panemone: Vertical Axis Wind Turbine
Pelton Wheel: Micro-Hydro Electricity Generator
Spa pool: Solar Heated
Various Hot Water systems: Solar Heated, Thermonuclear powered.
Steam Engine: Powered by a Solar Furnace
Tri-cycle: Solar and human powered
All these and much more information can be viewed on their web site.
www.users.actrix.co.nz/albie.fill

We enjoyed a lovely supper and later attended a Meeting for Worship and presented the Quaker story. They really appreciated the bucket of 49 mussels we left with them! We had yet another wonderful experience.

West Coast Journey to Fox's Glazier
Monday, 2 April and it was officially autumn. The day before the clocks had been turned back an hour. We could certainly feel the cooler air, especially in the evenings and early mornings. After our informative stay with our farming friends, and yet again such wonderful hospitality, we left Golden Bay heading south back along State Highway 60 to Motueka, then turned off taking a bye road through Pokororo and Woodstock (pulled over here to listen to a little music!). We then joined State Highway 6 at Kobatu travelled onto Murchison and through Bullers Gorge to Westport for the night. That much used word "amazing" couldn't possibly describe the scenery as we drove along this route.

The roads were slow in the campervan due to the twists and turns, but wow the views and landscapes were tremendous. It's a country where you travel along and say "oh wow", and then turn a corner and there's an even bigger "Oh wow". The lush hillsides with their different colours of green were beginning to be tinged with hues of brown as autumn was approaching. The ferns and fauna were amazing. The rippling waters and the different shades of blue were astounding.

We hooked up for the night in Westport and I spent the evening frantically trying to finish our knitted gloves in readiness for our glacier walk.

Gloves completed and after a good night's rest we carry on heading south from Westport to Greymouth. We didn't stop at Greymouth as we had visited there in December, we travelled on down to Hokitika. We pulled up for a tea stop just north of Hokitika and decided to have an early lunch and then off down the road again. This was quite a long stint, as all our extra visits to various places had left us a tad short of time. We were due to return Isaac the week before flying back to England on 24 April, but there was still so much we wanted to see and do. We eventually pulled over in a layby to have a break from travelling. It was lovely, peaceful and quiet even with the occasional noise of the passing traffic, so we made use of our two folding chairs.

Quite suddenly Bill jumped out of his seat and I nearly choked on my food as he said, "Don't move, stay perfectly still, sshhh!"

What a stupid thing to say to me! I was up in a minute and into the van with the door slammed behind me. When I peered out of the window, Bill was stood with one hand on his hip glaring at me, and the other hand pointing to a small brown head peeping out of the bush.

"What?" I gave him one of my looks. "It's a bird, what's the fuss?".

When it eventually fully appeared, it was about the size of a bantam hen but longer from beak to tail.

I quietly opened the door and stepped out to be told again, "ssshhh!"

What had he expected me to do. The way he'd jumped I thought there was a snake or something horrible coming out of the bush, or maybe Mr. Nippy Tail had hitched a lift with us again. Vivid imagination or just tired? Bill would go with the former. In quite a loud whisper, normal voice to me, but to Bill it's a whisper, he said, "At last I've got you."

Before he could carry on I said, "Don't you dare, there's no way I'm cooking that tonight."

To which he replied, "No don't be silly. It's Mr. Weka. I've been watching for him for hours, get the camera quick."

It was his first sighting of the weka, known as the wood hen, and he was grinning like the cat that got the cream, Bill not the bird. He later explained to me, after I'd taken many photos of Mr. Weka, that it's a flightless bird and suffers from imported predators, rats, weasels, stoats, possums, as well as cats and dogs in peopled areas. Its southern most boundary on the west coast was Hokitika, so we were in the last few kilometers of possibly seeing one. Bill sat there mesmerized and delighted. Ticked that box again.

We hit the road again with a very cheerful Bill, and made our way down to Franz Josef glazier. We hadn't really decided which of the glaciers we would walk, but when we arrived at the Franz Josef we continued onwards. We looked bemused at each other, then when we thought about it, of course it had to be Fox's Glacier didn't it! Although Bill had a different explanation.

"Yes, I'm not surprised you've driven past the first glacier. No doubt it's going to be like parking at the supermarket, when you drive round and round looking for a space and I keep saying there, there, but no, you just drive round and round."

I just thought to myself, did someone speak?

We arrived at the township of Fox's Glacier in mid-afternoon on Tuesday, 3 April and yes, I did eventually park up. We settled for a cabin at the holiday park, as it was getting quite cold in the evenings, no heating in the van and only summer duvets, well, that was my excuse.

The glaciers form an obvious connection between the coast and the highest peaks of the Southern Alps. At 13 kilometres Fox's Glacier is the longest of the awe-inspiring New Zealand west coast glaciers. At its head, soaring peaks of over 3,000 metres dominate the vista. These include Aoraki (Mt Cook) and Mt Tasman. This mighty moving river of ice falls 2,600 metres on its journey from the base of the Southern Alps to the west coast. New Zealand's west coast glaciers are unique and probably the most accessible glaciers in the world, as they terminate amongst temperate rainforest approximately 300 metres above sea level. Glaciers are held in delicate balance by the accumulation of snow gained in the upper glacier and ice melting in the lower part. Fox's Glacier is fed by four alpine glaciers which have approximately 30 metres of snowfall every year.

Kea Parrot in Action

We planned to book the glacier walk the next morning. It was a warmer than usual evening, surprising really, as we were sat just a few kilometers below Fox's Glacier. We'd enjoyed a simple evening meal and were sat outside the cabin watching the kea parrots screeching and flying around the site. There were quite a few of these noisy birds, flying in and out of the trees and then hopping about on the ground, looking for anything they could get their beaks into. There was a Kea camper van, this was the name of the campervan company, not a campervan for keas, but we did eventually wonder, parked a little way from our cabin. Three or four of the birds perched on top of the van and we were laughing saying,

"Oh, they know which is their van, what clever birds."

They didn't come anywhere near ours or any of the other vans on the site. They waddled around the roof of the van, looking all over the sides and then the fun began. The occupants of the van were sat below enjoying a quiet drink, when suddenly the birds started to rip and pull at the rubber strips around the van. Oh boy, did they know what they were doing! They were pulling and tugging going to town on it. We sat in amazement. Couldn't believe it, even though we had been told they would tear anything to shreds, but a campervan? The occupants of the van were alerted and out came the long-handled brushes, or whatever else they could find to try and see the birds off, with some success. The birds flew off, back into the trees, but no sooner had the occupants sat down again than the birds were back. This time the occupants sat outside to keep an eye on the van and the birds. How clever the kea birds were as two of them landed ever so quietly onto the roof of the van and peered over the edge. It was unreal, they were watching the occupants whilst carefully and quietly stripping the van. We alerted the people once again and with brushes in hand they repeated their shooing actions. The birds left and didn't come back immediately, so the occupants obviously decided it was safe to go off the site. They must just have turned the corner when the birds came back and they ripped and pulled at the rubber for a good 30 minutes, nothing was going to deter them. Everyone walking past tried to shoo them away, including us but they weren't giving up at all. They were pulling the cables out and stripping any rubber they could get their beaks around.

How would you explain to the Kea Campervan Company that there's no rubber or cable left on top of the van because your own birds, the kea parrots, stripped it off?

The following morning, we signed up for a half-day trip to Fox's Glacier. When we arrived, we were kitted out by the guide company with mountain boots, socks and wet weather jackets, with an option of a knapsack and had it been wet, over trousers. Oh, don't forget we had our own gloves newly knitted by 'moi'. Bills' were bright green and mine a nice burgundy colour. We were then briefed as to how the morning would go and bussed out to within one kilometre of the glacier. Once there we set off up the valley towards the glacier, it was a good walk although at a very gentle pace. We took lots of photographs and enjoyed the time it took to get to the snout of the glacier, and then up onto the surface of the glacier and the climb began. There was a path leading up to the snout where you could get a reasonable view of it, but it was recommended that it was guided parties only beyond that point for safety sake. Some people in the past had ignored this advice and had been quite seriously injured!

In front of us, and working very hard, were guides cutting fresh steps into the glacier to make easier access for the guided parties. The glacier moves about 50cm a day and the sun induced run off water makes it necessary for new steps to be formed each morning. One of our group had friends, who were paying three times as much as we had to have a helicopter trip over the glaciers, but she reckoned she had the better deal. We trudged up the glacier with some slipping and sliding, but it was a terrific experience. We had a great time and felt it was very good value for money. It was invigorating and fresh, a complete contrast to being on the beach a few days earlier. We were pretty pooped by the time we got back to the campsite, as we did walk quite a long way up the glacier, so we reckoned it had been just the right amount of time for the energy we had.

We were back at the site and having a relaxing afternoon, when back they came, the kea birds! They were determined to strip the Kea van of all its rubber and cables, how did they know it was one of theirs? Yet again, they didn't go near any other vans on the site.

www.foxguides.co.nz

Chapter 21

Southern Alps and a Real Scottish Castle

We left Fox's Glacier on the Thursday morning and joined State Highway 6 down the west coast to Haast where we turned inland to follow the Haast river road, which turns south and climbs up the Haast Pass. The east part of the Haast Valley road was a classical glaciated area, which had been reworked by the once massive river coming out of the Southern Alps. There was a big wide riverbed with multiple gravel and stone banks with waterways in between them. It would have been spectacular to see it in full flood, but I don't think the folks living along its course would have been too happy.

Once over the pass the road turned south along the Makarora River and arrived at the end of Lake Wanaka. We travelled down along the lake to Wanaka town and found a good campsite for the night.

Lanarch Castle

On Good Friday, we were back on the road again and drove past the Wanaka annual air show site, which had a wonderful line of old and new planes in a field beside the road. We were heading back to the Dunedin area, after all, we'd promised to revisit Dorothy and Eli. So, we took State Highway 8a and 8, south to the east side of Lake Dunstan and on to Cromwell. There was lots of fine scenery all the way, mountains with snow, giving way to bare hills, and wonderful rocky areas, from forest to sheep and cattle pastures. We followed the Clutha River, through the township of Clyde with its hydro station. Alexandra, Roxburgh and the rest of Scotland, only it wasn't. It reminded us of somewhere in the glens or the borders only more of it, higher hills, wider glens, but still sparsely populated, and difficulty finding a café open for a cuppa, although we could have made our own. We'd planned to stopover again before reaching Dunedin but Isaac just would not stop! Onward, onward, droned the eighteen hundred, (that was his engine size), until he reached the coastal plain and Milton township, but still no cup of tea! We gasped into Dunedin and made our way to a lovely campsite at Portobello, on the Otago Peninsula, where we made tea….at last.

After a peaceful night, we wanted to do something touristy and found Lanarch Castle, just a slight detour after leaving Portobello campsite. We visited the castle before going back to Dorothy and Elis' for the evening.

The History of Lanarch Castle

Lanarch Castle is an imposing mansion on the ridge of the Otago Peninsula. It was built in 1871 by William James Lanarch and was apparently New Zealand's only genuine castle. William Lanarch began a career in banking in Melbourne, but during the gold rush years he took up the position of Manager of the Bank of Otago in Dunedin in the 1860s. His career continued with his merchant empire 'Gutherie and Lanarch,' banking, shipping, farming, landholding, politics and speculation. He married three times and had six children. It is said that William Lanarch rode along the top of the Otago Peninsula and chose the site for Lanarch castle. With spectacular and panoramic views across to Dunedin, Otago Harbour, the Peninsula and the Pacific Ocean, it must have seemed idyllic. Materials from all over the world were used in the building of it along with some natural woods from New Zealand, one being the kauri tree. After three successive wives and the loss of his favourite daughter, Lanarch took his own life in New Zealand's House of Parliament. The family were torn apart by the legal battle that followed and the castle was sold in 1906. The castle then had many owners and became a lunatic asylum, a hospital for shell-shocked soldiers, and a nun's retreat.

In 1967 Margaret and Barry Barker bought Lanarch Castle. They have spent many years restoring and developing the castle and gardens into the glorious place it is today.

The Gardens were beautiful and contained a Rain Forest Garden, a Patterned Garden, the Lost Rock Garden, the South Seas Garden, the Serpentine Walk and the Alice Lawn along with figures from Alice in Wonderland hidden amongst the trees and bushes. There was also a Methane Gas Generation Plant. The inside of the castle was very interesting and cleverly restored. The rooms were quite open with no ropes protecting valuables or furniture, which was refreshingly trusting of the family. All the proceeds from visitors were being used for the restoration and maintenance of the buildings and grounds. The Barker family had done a fantastic job saving a major part of Dunedin's heritage and contributing to local tourism.
www.lanarchcastle.co.nz

Goodbye to friends in Dunedin

We later joined Dorothy and Eli for a Thai meal and stayed the night at their home, it was a lovely evening. The next morning, being Easter Sunday, there was an Ecumenical Easter Morning service on the top of Mount Cargill at 6.30 a.m. We joined other locals, and although it was quite windy and very cold, it was lovely to drive to the top of the mountain and see the views along with the sunrise. It was a special service for us as we were coming towards the end of our wonderful New Zealand experience, what better way to do this than sharing it with friends and local people.

After the service, we shared a scrumptious breakfast at the Methodist church. Sadly, it was soon time to say our tearful and final farewells to Dorothy and Eli. They had been such fantastic hosts. They hadn't seemed to mind us popping in and out of their lives. We will be forever grateful for their hospitality and companionship as well as tales of home.

As I'm driving away, with tears in my eyes, someone started to sing. "♪ On the road again ♪," that soon put a stop to the tears, he was still out of tune, so I gritted my teeth and put my foot down. Reminder to myself, must get Bill singing lessons on our return home. That's if he gets that far!

Chapter 22

The Church of the Good Shepherd

Lake Tekapo
There was one place that we really wanted to see, but time was marching on. We had felt that we'd rushed down the west coast of the South Island, but then we had changed our schedule so many times we couldn't have it all ways! I think if we had stayed in New Zealand for years, we wouldn't have seen all the wonders it has to offer. There had been so many we had sacrificed but we couldn't possibly let the next one slip past us. Lake Tekapo and the Church of the Good Shepherd.

The name derived from the Maori taka (sleeping mat) and po (night), suggesting that it had been used as a stopover for many years. It is also reputed to have the clearest air in the southern hemisphere at an altitude of 710 metres, and again the water reflects the usual glacial turquoise hue that's found in so many of the rivers and lakes in this area. It was quite dramatic with the mountainous background of the Southern Alps.

We made our way north to Timaru, where we branched off west and followed State Highway 8 to Lake Tekapo. There was still yet more wonderful countryside, with amazing views. Close to Lake Tekapo we crossed a level area that was a bit desert like, with Tekapo River in the distance. By this time, it was getting quite late and we had seen the sun set and darkness began to fall. We hadn't thought it would be very busy, as it was out of the summer season, but of course we'd forgotten about the Easter break. So, we trudged along confident we'd get a hook up. We really struggled. Never mind a hook up we couldn't get onto the first couple of sites at all, so we motored onto Lake Tekapo itself.

We arrived to find a very busy and bustling evening at Lake Tekapo. Restaurants were doing a roaring trade and there was a throng of people wandering around this tiny village. We later discovered that a lot were possibly day-trippers, who hadn't left for their return journey home or their next destination. We eventually found a tent site, which we were allowed to stay on overnight. But, by then it was quite dark and we carefully backed up in amongst some pine trees unable to see very much around us. Eventually we got our bearings, or at least Bill did, and had a wander down to the village to look for somewhere to eat, as it would have been difficult to cook in the van with such limited light. I'm pretty useless at orientation in the daylight, so I wouldn't have much hope in the dark!

The next morning, we packed up and set off to see the Church of the Good Shepherd.

A Church with a View

The church was built in 1935 for the pioneer families of the Mackenzie District. The early run holders of this district risked their lives in the hills around there caring for their sheep.

They understood the words of Jesus the Christ when he said,

"I am the good shepherd. I know my sheep as the Father knows me. So, I give my life for my sheep. I also have other sheep that are not from this pen. I must lead them. They, too, will respond to my voice. So, they will be one flock with one shepherd. The greatest love you can show is to give your life for your friends."

From the Gospel of John; Chapter 10 - verses 7 to 16 and Chapter 15 - verse 13.

(As printed on the leaflet from the church).

The altar window frames a spectacular view across the lake towards the mountain range beyond. The blue lake rippled and the mountains in the distance cast their shadows on the chrystal clear water. We enjoyed a peaceful few minutes, as we sat in the pews, in silence.

The church had become an iconic tourist attraction, which somewhat detracted from the tranquility of it as it sat on the edge of Lake Tekapo. Obviously, we had been part of that disturbance. Sorry, Good Shepherd.

About 100 metres east of the church was the Collie Dog monument. Local sheep farmers had erected the monument in 1968 to honour the dogs that made it possible to graze the harsh terrain.

What a wonderful start to the day, but, it was soon time to leave as we had a 3-hour journey ahead of us back to Christchurch. We felt quite humbled and travelled the first part of the journey in our own quiet worlds.

Chapter 23

Christchurch - an Earthquake Experience

We arrived back in Christchurch, and of course where else would we spend our last days in this area but Amber Park. We booked into one of the tourist flats, as we would be using Isaac at the weekend to go to our final camp, and so we needed to catch up on chores etc.

It was Thursday, 12 April 2012 and we were preparing to go into the suburb of Riccarton to do some final shopping. We'd just finished lunch. I was sat at the table sorting some of our papers and checking everything was in order for our flight home. Yes, I am always way ahead of myself. Bill was stood looking at me and was grumbling, quite exasperated.

He became impatient as he said, "Stop being so organized, you can do that another day."

I decided to annoy him even more with the last word, no, song.

"We're leaving on a jet plane don't know when we'll be back again do de do do da."

Bill turned and glared at me. My singing came to an abrupt end, as suddenly, my chair started to move and shake around. It was quite forceful. I grabbed hold of the table and it was moving too.

I looked up at Bill as he screwed his face up and said, "What on earth are you doing?"

I nervously replied, "Can't you feel that?"

I'd no sooner got the last word out when Bill put his hands to his head and groaned, "Oh, oh no, no!"

We were both caught off guard and didn't make a move to get out of the building, which we should have done. Then it stopped. We looked at one another in confusion. I gulped and caught my breath.

"Right, if it starts again we get outside." I pushed the papers back into the envelope and grasped my bag ready for the off.

What were we waiting for? I thought.

We didn't move and all was eerily quiet. We then came to our senses and headed out of the building. People were stood around in the car park looking relieved, as it wasn't another biggy. I felt the movement straight away but there had been a few seconds time lapse before Bill felt anything. He later described it as though something had shivered up through his body to his head, which made his head feel like lead and too heavy to hold up. It was still pretty scary, even though our brains hadn't comprehended what was happening straight away. It had been a 4.6 earthquake and we knew there would be a lot of very frightened people around especially the children, as they never get used to them, after all the next could be another big one.

We decided to carry on with our plans and go shopping to Riccarton. Once there we were quite shocked. Since our last visit more buildings had been damaged, and there was yet more fencing around a lot of the shops.

I met a young woman whilst out shopping and she said, "Did you feel the quake?"

I said, "Yes." I told her how it had taken us by surprise and we didn't quite get what was happening at first. I asked her if everyone was all right.

She replied, "Well, I rang the school and the children are safe. My husband has texted me and he is safe. But when I get home, I don't know what I'll find. We're trying to keep our home as normal as possible, for the children, but we do have to tie things down. Nothing is normal anymore."

We had discussed how we must stay safe, but this new experience had made us more aware of any movement or noise, and that we should be better prepared to make a move. How could you ever comprehend the effect the daily quakes and aftershocks were having on the community. It was just so intense.

Some of the comments from the people of Christchurch:

"The after-shocks are still unexpected, they come when we least expect them.

Now and then we're lulled into a false sense of security. But, deep down, under the surface, the fear is always there, and when the earth quakes again we hope and pray that it won't be another big one.

There is little respite, this is reality! Our world has been turned upside down. Our children are scared.

We continue with our daily tasks, but without the security we once had. We find it difficult to focus on anything for long, it's like having a permanently 'foggy' brain. Here it comes again! The room shakes and we run to find the safest place. Will our lives ever be normal again?"

Chapter 24

Isaac's Last Stand

Camping, Tramping and Funny Stories
On Friday, 13 April we joined seven Friends from Christchurch Meeting at Craigieburn Environmental Education Centre for a tramping weekend. It was to be our final weekend with Isaac. There were bunk beds in the centre but we opted out, and decided to stay with our faithful friend, Isaac. It seemed to be an overshadowed site upon our arrival that evening. But later it became sunny, as the sun came up over the trees and hills surrounding the centre. In the evening, we enjoyed a shared meal and talked about the events in Christchurch, and our different lives.

Saturday's tramp for us was along a well-used path to a saddle between two valleys, where we walked through the mountain beech forest. We then had an option to go up a hill next to the saddle called Helicopter Hill, or stay on the lower tracks. We chose Helicopter Hill, which was a climb along a steep ridge over open screes. This was the exhilarating bit, as it was steep and rocky as we climbed up and out of the tree line. We arrived on the top to find the sun had appeared, which enhanced the 360° views across the surrounding mountains and valleys. We strolled around for a while admiring the breathtaking views, then sat for a few minutes in awe of the magnificent vista. We took some fantastic photographs and then descended to rejoin those who hadn't climbed to the summit.

Later we had a 'jolly' shared evening meal and spent a couple of hours afterwards sharing tales and laughing a lot. It was such good fun sharing stories. Our fellow trampers rolled about laughing as I shared a story about Bill and a train journey.

"We'd been working at Swarthmoor Hall and Bill had to attend a conference. The hall was fully booked with a weekend event, and I could only manage to get one volunteer for a short stint. By the

Sunday afternoon I was fairly whacked. I was so glad Bill was due back later that afternoon and I could hand over to him.

He rang me from Birmingham train station and said he'd ring when he arrived in Lancaster, at which point he said, "I must dash there's a train leaving soon for Edinburgh if I jump on that it'll get me back all the sooner."

Excellent, I thought, and settled down to a cup of tea, before continuing with the clearing up that was facing me.

About an hour later I answered the 'phone again. It was Bill. I thought, no, he can't be at Lancaster already.

"Hi, sorry," he said, "oh dear I'm going to be later than I thought, wrong train it was going up the east coast instead of the west coast."

"Oh," I said. "Good job you didn't get on it then"

"Mmm," he said, "I did."

"What? What do you mean?" I replied

"Well, I got on the train, left Birmingham and then they announced calling at Sheffield, and I thought why would we go via Sheffield? Oh, well, never mind. Then they came to look at my ticket, and informed me, quite briskly, that I was on the wrong train. Oh blimey! I hadn't thought about it, so I've been part way up the east coast and back down again."

Then without drawing breath and as though nothing had happened he said, "Right there's a train due in 20 minutes, ring you from Lancaster, bye" and the line went dead. I was left stood there looking at the 'phone and wondering if I'd really had that conversation.

Several hours later Bill rang again. This time he was in Lancaster and would be getting the next train and would be due back in about an hour, so I would meet him at the station.

I left the chores I hadn't managed to finish and went to the station to collect Bill, relieved he was back and another pair of hands to help with the work. I didn't usually get out of the car and go onto the platform but on this occasion, I did. The train pulled in and I looked along to see where he was. He was there, sitting in a window seat. So, I went over to the train and knocked on the window, Bill looked up and waved and then carried on writing in his notebook.

What! I thought. I knocked on the window again and said, "Are you getting off?"

He looked up again and said, "Hello."

To which I replied, "Are you getting OFF?"

The look of astonishment on his face was unbelievable, he jumped up, gathered his belongings and ran down the train just as the train manager was about to blow the whistle.

As he alighted I shouted to him, "Where are your display boards?"

The train manager looked totally confused, as Bill jumped back on the train and ran down the passageway to retrieve his display boards.

Panic over. All present and correct and in the car.

As I was driving away I asked, "What were you doing, you just waved, what was that all about?"

"Well," Bill replied, "I was writing poetry and then I saw you and thought, oh look, there's Sylvia and gave you a wave, my mind was elsewhere".

"Writing poetry! Writing poetry! Well I've heard it all now, writing poetry." I said in disbelief.

On relating this story to the group, and of course with some slight exaggeration, they all fell about laughing and so the stories continued and we giggled and belly laughed our way through the evening. The next morning, we packed up, cleaned up and had a lovely worship session together then headed back to Christchurch.

We checked back into Amber Park into a tourist flat as Isaac was going home the next day, Monday. We had a lot of sorting and cleaning to do before we returned him. Oh, how we would miss him, our ever-faithful friend.

Later in the evening I was cooking in the campsite kitchen. Busying herself beside me was a young Japanese girl. We exchanged the usual greetings and how long we had both been travelling as best we could understand each other.

She then asked me, "What you do in evenings as long time travel? Oooh, six months, long time travel."

So, I explained, "Well, we're never bored, we can sit outside and watch the sunset and then star gaze up into the sky. If the weather isn't too good we read or update our blog, you know that sort of thing."

She looked at me and nodded. I by this time had forgotten she could probably only understand about half of what I was saying.

I carried on, "Oh but lately we've been watching 'Cold Feet' on the lap top, we missed it the first time around on the TV in England."

Before I could say anything else she looked sad and said, "Oh, very sorry, you have cold feet," as she looked down at my bare sandaled feet.

"Maybe you cover them, not watch them, cover them, then they get better." Before I could reply her partner entered the kitchen and they chattered in Japanese for a couple of minutes. She then pointed down to the floor, and they both looked at my feet.

I was just about to try to explain to them when Bill burst through the door and said, "Oh great the foods ready, let me help you carry it to the van."

The couple are still looking at my feet and Bill looked down and said, "What's wrong, not Mr. Nippy Tail again?"

"No," I replied, and started to explain that I was trying to tell them that I didn't have cold feet and that it was a TV programme.

At which point Bill held his hand up, gave the Japanese couple a lovely big smile and said, "No cold feet, she ok, she warm feet, she ok."

Bill then proceeded to gently push me and the food through the door and followed very close behind. Looking back and smiling at the couple he then said to me, in a rather loud voice, "No more 'Cold Feet' for you. It's Miranda tonight!"

Thanks Miranda Hart you made us laugh and feel jolly after a pretty challenging day.

Goodbye Isaac our Faithful Friend

Monday morning arrived and it was quite sad, as we were to say our farewells to Isaac and return him to the depot in Christchurch. He had served us tremendously well on our travels throughout both Islands of New Zealand. I had become very fond of him, in fact, I could have brought him home with me! He looked very handsome, all spruced up after we'd washed, cleaned and tidied him, (and even combed his hair), so he was very presentable when we took him back to the hire company. We said a very sad goodbye to Isaac and took a hire car for the next eight days, although it had caused some friction between us, as most of the hire cars were automatic. I didn't mind but Bill wasn't keen after his experience with the automatic car at the beginning of our adventure. So, I opted to drive, oh well in for a penny and all that. We hired a lovely little car, a Nissan Colt, very nippy travelling in and out of the city. I actually enjoyed the freedom of driving an automatic.

The Giant's House

We had a couple of days at a friend's section, where we helped do some weeding, fruit bush and tree pruning. We then moved on and decided our final adventure would be back in Akaroa. We booked a cabin for a couple of nights at Little River about half way between Christchurch and Akaroa. We took our final trip into Akaroa as we had wanted to see the Giant's House, which we'd missed on our previous visit to the area, and we definitely didn't want to miss a kumara fish meal. Unfortunately, the renowned chip shop we had hoped to buy our fish and chips from had burnt down a couple of weeks previously. We stood staring at the charred remains somewhat shell shocked or probably just hungry! We searched about the town and found another wee café, Trudy's sea front café, where we had an excellent fish and chip lunch.

We visited the Giant's House, what a wonderful place to stroll around on a lovely sunny autumn afternoon. The garden had been sculptured and gardened in a rather crazy and unusual way. It was an historic house, and had been the home of the first bank manager of Akaroa, built in 1880 with totara and kauri wood. Designed and decorated in a French style, it was the home of Josie Martin, a mixed media artist, sculptress, horticulturist and traveller. There was bed and breakfast accommodation available in the house with large bedrooms, quirky bathrooms and unique artistic features throughout.

It had a terraced garden, which was full of surprises with mosaic steps, a sculptured wall mosaic, welded steel sculptures covered with fragments of pottery, glass and ceramics.

It was like being in a fairytale garden. The general feel was that of a cross between Gaudi (Barcelona) and Hundertwasser. We explored it all, then sat for a while, soaking it all in and enjoying a typical, big, New Zealand ice cream. Hokey Pokey for me and a crazy mixture of flavours for (crazy) Bill!

We were coming to the end of our journey and would spend the last few days in Christchurch. We stayed just on the outskirts of the city near the Groynes recreational domain, as we wanted to get quite a few good walks in before our long flight home. We walked daily through the bush and around a big lake, where Bill could still watch the birds, there were lots of mallard ducks and other water fowl. There were fantails like we'd never seen them before dancing along the paths. It took us back to when Bill was rushing through the bush, binoculars to his eyes, like someone crazed, trying to catch sight of the bellbird, and there now was the fantail flitting in and out of the bush as though teasing poor Bill.

Farewell

We made our final visit into Christchurch centre, that is as far as we possibly could, and were amazed at how the damage had spread further and further outwards towards the suburbs. We went to the Botanic Gardens, but were left quite saddened as by this time a lot of it was closed off. The conservatory and glass houses had been closed due to previous damage and the risk of ongoing earthquakes. However, we had a good walk around and sat in the sun enjoying a picnic lunch. The quakes didn't seem to deter people from doing their usual stuff. There were lots of families around, playing and enjoying the autumn sunshine, and generally having a good time.

It was soon Sunday and our final Meeting for Worship with Christchurch Friends followed by a splendid shared lunch. There was a good discussion session after lunch around the theme of the Business Meeting, which we attended and facilitated the last part. We eventually said our farewells, and extended an invitation to anyone from the Meeting to get in touch with us if they were in the UK and needed help. We also encouraged them all to visit the North West and 1652 country.

Our tramping friends from the previous weekend had announced how much they had enjoyed our company, wished we were staying longer, as they'd hardly gotten to know us. They regaled how they hadn't laughed so much for such a long time, as we told our tales, in fact to the point of tears.

And so, the time had come, with some sadness we were leaving for home.

We said our final goodbyes with Tears, Love and Laughter.

Farewell.

E noho rā   Goodbye

Bill and Sil's 101 Favourite Travel Experiences
1. Chinese food in a Hawker Centre, Singapore
2. Singapore Botanical Gardens
3. Chinatown and the Buddha Tooth Relic Temple
4. Christchurch a devastated city
5. Our faithful friend Isaac
6. Kumara Supper in Akaroa
7. Container Shopping Mall, Christchurch
8. Bonfire night at New Brighton
9. Thermal pools at Hanmer Springs
10. Flaxmere Gardens
11. Meeting Friends in Sumner
12. Yellow Eyed and Blue Penguins in Oamaru
13. Steam Punk Engine
14. Moeraki Boulders
15. A night in Trotters Gorge
16. Savouring a New Zealand sausage roll.
17. Orokonui Eco Sanctuary, Dunedin
18. Sailing on the Milford Sound
19. Meeting ET at the Chasm
20. Flowers that are treasured in the UK, but are classed as noxious weeds in New Zealand
21. Sharing lunch with the kea parrot
22. The beauty of Lake Te Anau
23. Walkways around Lake Manapouri
24. Driving across the longest bridge in New Zealand
25. Invercargill
26. The Royal Albatross Centre, Taiaroa Head
27. TranzAlpine train journey
28. A Christmas Carol Service in the summer
29. Whale watching in Kaikaura
30. Seals posing on the rocks
31. Stay overnight at Grassmere Lake in New Zealand
32. False snow in Blenheim
33. Wine tasting in Marlborough
34. Sailing the sea from Picton to Wellington
35. Staying at the Whanganui Quaker settlement

36. Summer snow on the top of Mount Egmont
37. Scouring the beach in the dark at Waiiti
38. Waitomo Valley and caves
39. Christmas lunch Al fresco at Miranda
40. The crimson red flowers of the Pohutukawa Christmas tree
41. The Chosen Valley
42. Meeting our Kiwi family
43. Taste Manuka honey, the best in New Zealand
44. Visiting Galbraith's, the pub that brewed its own beer.
45. The magnificent Kauri museum
46. Meeting 'The Father of the Forest'
47. Walking the boardwalks among the mangroves
48. Cape Reigna the furthest point on the North Island
49. Listening for the Spirits leap at Spirit Bay
50. The Treaty of Waitangi
51. Seeing the fossil forest at Takapuna
52. A convenience made from broken tiles, bricks and glass
53. Sitting in a Giant's chair
54. Algie's Castle
55. The drive up the Coromandel Peninsula
56. Digging for hot water and bathing on the beach
57. Body boarding on paradise
58. Getting lost in the World War II tunnels
59. Hamilton Garden Festival
60. Thermal steam and the Rotorua Museum
61. A Maori Experience
62. Middle Earth - Hobbiton
63. Walking up to the top of a volcanic crater
64. An inventive corrugated town
65. Visiting an information centre in the shape of a sheep
66. Sending a wooden postcard
67. Buying a Paua shell
68. Seeing the abundance of Jade stones
69. Visiting a wonderful privately owned vintage museum
70. Experiencing an artificial earthquake/volcanic eruption
71. Lake Taupo
72. The frothing Aratiatia Rapids

73. The Huka Falls
74. Enjoying a Hangi cooked meal
75. Checking out a steam fuelled town
76. Relaxing in thermal pools
77. The Museum of Wellington
78. Watching the dolphins leap the bow currents
79. Driving around the Queen Charlottte Sound
80. Staying on an eco-site
81. Nelson
82. Walking on an island of Easter bunnies
83. Going underground to see the skeleton of a flightless bird
84. Finding the Split Apple
85. Gathering mussels
86. Watching the kea bird strip the rubber off a camper van
87. Walking along a glacier
88. Meeting Mr. Weka
89. Travelling through Scotland in New Zealand
90. The church of the Good Shepherd
91. Lake Tekapo
92. Lanarch Castle
93. Big Hokey Pokey New Zealand ice cream
94. Talking to the locals
95. Bill's Birds
96. Walking the bush to the top of Helicopter Hill
97. Visiting Little France
98. Amber Park, Chrischurch
99. Camping on a DoC site
100. The incredible breathtaking scenery of New Zealand
101. Wonderful people, wonderful country

Bill's Birds
(Of the feathered variety)

Bill was quite excited at the prospect of seeing different types of birds in New Zealand and was intent on spotting as many different species as was possible. Just about everywhere we went Bill would appear with his bird book in one hand and binoculars in the other. He was often seen chasing through the bush and the trees in various forests throughout the Islands. He sometimes expected me to chase after him with my camera to try and snapshot every bird he spotted, alas, it was bad enough one of us racing around bumping into people and trees so that wasn't to be, but I did get some good snaps here and there.

Bill listed his birds and here they are: -

Australian Coot

Found their own way to New Zealand and can be seen throughout the country on large freshwater lakes but are most common on the North Island. They forage on marginal grasses and eat invertebrates and aquatic plants.

Australian Harrier

A bird of prey from Australia seen commonly in New Zealand, it can often be seen leisurely flying across open countryside. They will look for road kill animals or dead sheep.

Australian Magpie

Introduced from Australia they are white and black backed magpies. They can be seen on both Islands nesting in tall trees, but in gorse or hawthorn hedges in the Canterbury area.

Bar Tailed Godwit

These birds have a dark rump but no wing-bars. Only seen in the summer months, these migrant waders arrive in New Zealand each spring. By autumn the godwit prepares to return to their breeding grounds in the Artic.

Bellbird
This little elusive bird certainly led Bill astray! Found throughout New Zealand they have an olive-green plumage and their bell like tones can be heard long before they're spotted. They feed on insects and fruit and are a forest species.

Blackbird
As in Britain the blackbird can be found throughout New Zealand and feed on fruit and invertebrates.

Black Backed Gulls or Dominican Gull
Nest along coastal area in colonies, although often scavenge in land they're recognizable by their black back.

Black Billed Gull
More common on the South Island and mainly inland, they eat live prey as well as insects.

Black Shag
Feed mainly inland but in autumn and early winter they can be seen in their hundreds feeding and diving into sheltered tidal waters.

Black Swan
The black swan originates from Australia and can be seen on most lakes and estuaries

Blue Penguin
This is the smallest of all penguins. Their compact feathers are a metallic blue/grey in colour. They fish all day and can be seen coming home at night in rafts to feed their young chicks.

California Quail
A plump and stocky introduced game bird with a distinct plume on its head. Can be seen throughout the Islands and feed on plants and insects on scrub or cultivated lands.

Canada Goose
A North American bird seen mainly in Canterbury and the North Otago region.

Caspian Tern
The caspian is the largest tern, they fish in shallow waters and can be identified on both Islands.

Chaffinch
The chaffinch can be seen in gardens and remote forest areas it's the most common introduced bird. Usually found amongst trees and bushes. They feed on some fruits, insects, seeds and grains.

Dunnock
A small brown song bird from England mostly seen in the South of New Zealand, they feed on insects.

Eastern Rosella Parrot
Originates from Australia and can be seen mainly on the North Island usually in forests, farmland and urban areas.

Fantail
The fantail is very lively bird it will flit along in the bush beside you and then dart out, spread its lovely tail into a fan and then off again. Making it just about impossible to photograph. Most common in the forest and scrubland or where insects can be found.

Goldfinch
Quite common in large areas of both islands and can often be seen feeding on thistle heads.

Grey Warbler
Widespread throughout New Zealand and found in forests, scrubland and sheltered gardens. A lively bird that feeds on insects.

House Sparrow
This bird was introduced to New Zealand to help control pests on crops. It's common wherever there's food.

Kaka Parrot
This parrot is named after its call of kra-kra-kra. Inhabits native forest on the main islands and not so easy to find as the kea and definitely not as playful.

Kea Parrot
This is the worlds' largest Alpine parrot. Named after its call of kee-aaa kee-aaa; it's a very cheeky bird but fascinating to watch. They'll rip apart anything you leave lying around, rucksack, boots etc. They have a beautiful olive green plumage.

Kingfisher
Mostly seen on the North Island and has a variety of habitats including forests and coastal areas.

Kiwi
The national bird of New Zealand. These birds are flightless and dart in and out of the bush and are mainly nocturnal. It has a long beak and its wings are tiny hidden under the hair like plumage. We only managed to see one of these and that was in captivity.

Knot
Mainly found on sandy beaches or the northern harbour tidelines, salt marshes and coastal flats.

Little Shag
A small bird with a white breast most often seen on rocks with wings spread wide.

Mallard
From Britain and the United States and easy to recognize.

Morepork
We waited a long time to hear the morepork owl although we didn't actually see one. A nocturnal bird which may often be seen hunting at dusk. Their call is a distinctive "morepork" and can mainly be heard in parks and suburbs.

Myna Bird
A very common bird in the north of the North Island. Most likely to be spotted walking down the middle of the road. Small numbers feed on the foreshores but can often be seen on the back of sheep or cattle picking off ticks.

New Zealand Dotterel
Not easy to spot on sandy beaches as it scurries about. A threatened bird, mainly seen on the North Island.

New Zealand Pigeon
This bird has once again become established in the forests as it was protected after the Europeans led to its decrease. A large bird that feeds on leaves and fruit.

Paradise Shelduck
It was the green and orange/amber plumage that eventually enabled us to identify this bird as it is very like a goose only smaller.

Pied Oystercatcher
This bird has a long orange bill and only breeds on the South Island

Pied Shag
Mostly seen in Marlborough and the North Island it is the second largest of its kind in New Zealand.

Pied Stilt
Long bill, long legs. Can be seen near tidal estuaries and wetlands.

Pukeko
A big body with long legs and a somewhat nervous bird. Widespread among the swamps of New Zealand.

Red Billed Gull
Nests around coastal waters with the black billed gulls

Rock Pigeon
This is a feral and city pigeon that has originated from domestic strains and is gradually reverting back to the plumage of its wild ancestors. Around the Banks Peninsula, Hawkes Bay and Auckland they are largely feral and breed naturally in caves off coastal and inland cliffs.

Royal Albatross
One of the worlds' largest flying birds and breeds only in New Zealand. With a wingspan of up to 3 metres they glide majestically in the sky and can't be missed. They build their nests on the Otago Peninsula, Campbell, Auckland and the Chatham Islands.

Royal Spoonbill
A large heron like bird with a black spoon like bill and like the heron spends its time fishing in rivers and lake waters.

Silver Eye
Originates from Australia and can be seen in forest or gardens. It has a white/silver patch around the eyes and green and orange feathers.

Skylark
Introduced from Europe but now very common in New Zealand. Mainly seen in open countryside, sand dunes and subalpine herb fields.

Song Thrush
Originated from Europe and will survive in many different types of country. They feed on insects, berries and fruit.

Spotted Shag
Nests on cliffs on both islands and usually seen perched on rocks.

Spur winged Plover or Masked Lapwing
A heron like bird but with a yellow beak. Can be found in fields near root crops, riverbeds, lagoons, lake shores and sheltered coastline.

Starling
The European starling is abundant everywhere except dense bush and high altitudes. They can mimic other birds and are very noisy. They feed on worms, fruit and insects

Turkey
It seemed odd to see turkeys running around in the wild. They have become feral in some districts, are almost totally vegetarian and will roost in the trees at night.

Tui
Mainly seen in the forests or suburbia they have blue, green and bronze plumage with a tufty white throat. Its notes are very tuneful although often interspersed with coughs, wheezes and harsh calls.

Turnstone
These birds are artic breeders and prefer rough shorelines. They will turn seaweed and stones over with their beaks to feed.

Welcome Swallow
Common throughout both islands and usually seen on wetlands or by the shore. Can be recognized by a deeply forked tail and a bright chestnut neck and face.

White Faced Heron
This was quite a common sighting in various wetlands, estuaries and harbours.

White Fronted Tern
The commonest tern in New Zealand often seen on sandy headlands or sometimes ventures inland to lakes and rivers.

Wrybill
Seen in the Canterbury area nesting on river beds and winters in the north of the North Island. This bird took quite a while to identify.

Variable Oystercatcher
Mainly found on sandy beaches, breeds on both islands and is a rare wading bird

Yellow Eyed Penguin
Apparently, this is one of the worlds' rarest penguins and inhabits the south-east coast of the South Island. They build their nests some distance from each other and sometimes up to 750 metres inland. They can be seen coming ashore late afternoon.

The Quaker Story
(a condensed version as presented by Bill Shaw)

The relationship between King Charles 1 and Parliament had become strained which led to the outbreak of civil war in 1642. The governance of the country became lax thereafter until Oliver Cromwell took control. Because of this during the war years many new ideas on social organization and religion were talked about and practiced.

George Fox was born in Fenney Drayton in 1624. His parents were weavers and his father was known as 'Righteous Christer' and his mother had descended from the stock of protestant Martyrs, the Lago family. By the time he was eleven years old, it was said that he knew pureness and righteousness as his 'yea' was 'yea' and his 'nay' was 'nay'. He was later apprenticed to a shoemaker/grazier who also dealt in wool and sold cattle.

In 1643 at just 19 years old he left home and wandered around the Midlands and the South of England talking to priests, ministers and professors, but none of them could answer his troubled mind. He engaged with others of different religious persuasions, but was dissatisfied with these discussions which at times would turn into arguments.

After several years wandering he came to the view from within himself that there was 'that of God, Spirit, The Light' in everyone and that people should turn inwards to find their teacher, Jesus, who was part of that 'Inward Light'. He felt that priests, ministers and such were standing in the way of people seeking true Christianity and spoke against them and the organized church. At this time, George Fox realized he could not rely on any person to answer his condition but heard from within,

"There is one, even Christ Jesus, that can speak to thy condition" and after hearing this he said "My heart did leap for joy".

His other openings from within set the basis for Quakerism, which developed over the following ten years.

George Fox travelled around England in the late 1640s to 1652 preaching his view and tried to convince others. He had some success and some groups were established as 'settled meetings'.

In 1650 George Fox was put in Derby Gaol and in exchange for an early release was offered a Captaincy in the Parliamentary Army.

He refused and said he, "Lived in the virtue of that life and power that took away the occasions of all wars." The Parliamentary Commissioners tried several times again to get him to join the army but he steadfastly refused. He was released in 1652 and made his way north. Times were beginning to change. Cromwell had been appointed Captain General and Commander in Chief of all the forces of the Commonwealth and a year later brought an end to the Civil War.

In North Yorkshire at Balby near Doncaster, George Fox met 30 or so seekers, who became convinced by his ministry. This was important in the spread of the ministry in the early years as several of them were good speakers and all were led by the Spirit. There were those who gave a warm hospitality to Fox but there were also those that didn't and through choice he would often spend the night in a haystack or a hedgerow, so he was not beholden to anyone.

Fox later said that God had pointed the way to Pendle Hill. Pendle Hill in Lancashire more famous for the 'Pendle Hill Witches' than Quakerism. In his Journal, he stated that he climbed the hill with 'much ado'. Was this not only a physical 'ado' as he was climbing a grassy, possibly slippery hill with flat well-worn leather boots or was it perhaps an 'ado' in his mind and spirit? On top of the hill he had a vision and saw "a great people wearing white raiment by a riverside, waiting to be gathered to the Lord."

He continued his journey ministering along the way until he came to the town of Sedbergh. He arrived in May of 1652 and at the time it was the day of the Hiring Fair. A Hiring Fair was a day when employees lined up in the towns market place to be viewed by prospective employers. The time of the Hiring Fair meant there were a lot of people about and there was a large audience to preach to. There were people preaching in the church and he was invited to do the same but he refused to go into "the steeple house" and preached in the open air of the church yard. Amongst the large crowd that were listening to George Fox were many Westmorland Seekers and several of their leaders. He later made contact with the Seekers at the Briggflats community and was invited to speak at the Seekers gathering at Firbank Fell on 13th June, 1652.

In his typical way, he replied to the invitation saying, "I will wait on the Lord and do his bidding." Well, he was bidden by the Lord to go to Firbank Fell. Again, he preached in the open air, not in the little chapel there. He spoke from the top of a rock at Firbank Fell, now known as Fox's Pulpit, for over three hours to over a thousand Seekers. Many were convinced and the Quaker movement developed a mass membership, and more importantly an organized group in a relatively small geographical area, giving it strength to reach out.

The Inscription of 'Fox's Pulpit' at Firbank Fell reads:

'Let your Lives Speak'

"Here or near this rock George Fox preached to about one thousand Seekers for three hours on Sunday, June 13, 1652. Great power inspired his message and the meeting proved of first importance in gathering the Society of Friends known as Quakers. Many men and women convinced of the Truth on this fell and in other parts of the northern counties went forth through the land and overseas with the living word of the Lord enduring great hardships and winning multitudes to Christ"

George Fox then travelled to Swarthmoor Hall just outside Ulverston, now in the county of Cumbria. This large estate was owned by Judge Thomas Fell, who was vice-Chancellor of the County-Palatine of Lancaster, Chancellor of the Duchy Court of Westminster, and had been elected Member of Parliament for Lancaster in 1645. The house was known to be hospitable to travelling preachers and Fox was welcomed by the daughters of the Fell family, as their mother Margaret Fell was away, as was Judge Fell, on business. Margaret Fell returned home to hear of this travelling preacher from her daughters and asked George Fox to preach in the local church the next day. He replied as usual, that he would wait on the Lord and do his bidding. However, he says in his journal that he was asked by the Light to go to the church and preach.

He stood up after Minister Lampitt had finished preaching and was about to preach when a magistrate of the town, Thomas Storey, stood and told George to sit down and harangued him. Margaret Fell stood up and said she would like to hear George Fox speak.

In the 17th century a woman would not dare to stand and speak out in front of the important men of the Parish but Margaret Fell was no ordinary woman. She was a member of the gentry and her husband was a well-respected Judge, so no one was brave enough to deny her request. George Fox spoke and afterwards Margaret Fell realised she had been an outward Christian and not an inward Christian and broke down and cried. She was convinced and vowed to become an inward Christian and a Quaker.

George Fox later travelled to Aldingham Church where the priest encouraged his congregation to listen to this preacher. He was beaten up several times in this area and nearly lost his life as crowds stoned him.

Later George Fox met with Judge Thomas Fell, who we believe was convinced but he knew the consequences for him and his family if he became a follower. He stayed behind the scenes supporting Margaret and allowing her to use their money to help Quakers in distress and to hold Quaker meetings at Swarthmoor Hall.

Margaret Fell would frequently intercede in cases of persecution and arrest, often with petitions to parliament and later to the King.

Over the following two years the 'Valiant 60', Quaker Missionaries, went out from the Hall, travelling the country and preaching to convince more people. During this time Swarthmoor Hall became the centre of Quakerism.

Judge Fell died in 1658 and within weeks of his death Margaret Fell was arrested and taken to Dalton Castle. One of the group of people who informed the authorities that she was holding illegal Quaker Meetings was her own son George Fell. She was moved to Lancaster Gaol for three years and suffered forfeiture of her property for failing to take the oath and holding Quaker meetings in her home.

During Margaret Fells time in prison she continued with her Quaker work writing letters and pamphlets and sent messages to those Quakers who were ill or being persecuted. She also fought hard for the equality of the sexes and for women to minister.

In 1668 Margaret Fell was released by order of the King Charles II.

Margaret Fell and George Fox were married in Bristol, 11 years after the Judge's death. Throughout their marriage, they continued with the Quaker work spending long periods of time apart.

George Fox died in 1690 in London. Margaret Fox continued her work and died at Swarthmoor Hall in 1702 and was laid to rest at Sunbrick Burial ground near Ulverston.

Margaret Fell

It was in the midst of the blazing fires of persecution that Swarthmoor Hall became a place of safety, a place of love and compassion and indeed a place of support. Margaret Fell became known as the 'Mother of Quakerism'. She rallied for the Quaker movement whilst raising a large family and often running the estate in her husband's (Judge Fell's) absence. This continued, and her unyielding endurance surely gave Quakerism the solid foundation that allowed the movement to strengthen.

Margaret Fell will be remembered as an outstandingly strong woman of her time.

Quaker Meeting for Worship

Quakers do not have priests or hierarchy – it is believed that we should all have our own direct relationship with God; whatever you perceive that to be.

Quakers look for the 'Inner Light' for guidance in their spiritual lives and believe that there is that of 'God' in everyone and that we are all equal in the eyes of the Lord.

Where there are two or more people gathered together we may meet to worship in silence. We will quieten the body, mind and spirit and wait for that still small voice. We will look for the Light to lead us to our subconscious and beyond, we will look inwardly at our lives. As the silence deepens our thoughts and senses change.

Meeting for Worship is held in silence but vocal ministry is often given from those who feel moved by the spirit to speak. We are asked not to judge ministry as although it will not always make sense to you, it may be a poignant and helpful message to others.

Meeting for Worship usually lasts an hour and at the end two appointed people will shake hands, and others may follow suit. This is usually followed by tea and coffee and general chatting or maybe a shared meal.

Quakers work hard to let their lives speak and live out the testimonies into their daily lives.

Quakers relate to each other as Friends.

Advices and Queries 1: Take heed, dear Friends, to the promptings of love and truth in your hearts. Trust them as the leadings of God whose Light shows us our darkness and brings us to new life.

Epilogue

Christchurch is now in the process of being carefully re-built, where at all possible. As the earth calms its rage the people of this once 'beautiful garden city' are beginning to piece their lives back together. Christchurch Quaker Meeting has found new premises and are making plans to re-confirm their vision, and are restructuring the building to fulfil this vision. They will come together in the midst of a community that has suffered loss and pain. They will help one another on the road to recovery, from their shared traumatic experiences, with a gentle hand and a warm heart.

The natural world has the power to give and the power to take away. From the creatures of the land and the seas, to the beautiful snow topped mountains and the magnificent landscapes rolling across the country side. Flora and fauna abound as the trees and the shrubs reach towards the sky. We as humans should treasure that which is on loan to us, we are stewards rather than owners. The natural world gives us food and shelter, so we must learn to help Mother Nature and listen to her. We put our needs and wants first. We always want more. So, for our generation and generations to come we must learn to respect this natural world and only take what we need to ensure there will always be enough for everyone.

'Be patterns, be examples in all countries, places, islands, nations, wherever you come, that your carriage and life may preach among all sorts of people, and to them; then you will come to walk cheerfully over the world, answering that of God in everyone'.

George Fox, 1656.

Bibliography

The Rough Guide to New Zealand
Collins – Birds of New Zealand - Chloe Talbot Kelly
People, People, People – A Brief History of New Zealand by Stevan Edred-Grigg
The long White Cloud by William Pember Reeves
Souvenir Guide Waitangi Treaty Grounds
The New Zealand Chronicle (Collector's Edition)
New Zealand History on line
On the Trans-Alpine Trail by Geoffrey Churchman
Advices and Queries

View our blog 'Bill and Sil's Amazing Zealand Adventure' with hundreds of outstanding photographs.

Printed in Great Britain
by Amazon